CHILDREN'S
ENCYCLOPEDIA
OF SCIENCE
EXPERIMENTS

Thomas Canavan

ARCTURUS

Having Fun and Being Safe

Inside this book you'll find a range of exciting science experiments that can be performed safely at home. Nearly all the equipment you need will be found around your own house. Anything that you don't have at home should be available at a local store. We have given some recommendations alongside the instructions to let you know when adult help might be needed. We would recommend close adult supervision for any experiment involving cooking equipment, sharp implements, electrical equipment, or batteries.

The author and publisher cannot take responsibility for any injury, damage, or mess that might occur as a result of attempting the experiments in this book. Always tell an adult before you perform any experiments, and follow the instructions carefully.

ARCTURUS

This edition published in 2020 by Arcturus Publishing Limited
26/27 Bickels Yard, 151–153 Bermondsey Street,
London SE1 3HA

Copyright © Arcturus Holdings Limited

Picture Credits: Every attempt has been made to clear copyright. Should there be any inadvertent omission, please apply to the publisher for rectification. All images from Shutterstock except p. 45 Design Pics Inc / Alamy Stock Photo, p. 59 Ivan Kuzmin / Alamy Stock Photo, p. 99 James Brey/Getty, p. 101 kozmoat98/Getty. All cover images from Shutterstock.

Author: Thomas Canavan
Designer: Lorraine Inglis
Picture Research: Paul Futcher and Lorraine Inglis
Illustrations: Joe Wilkins
Consultant: Elliott Josypenko
Copy Editor: Janet Bingham
Editor: Stephanie Carey
Managing Editor: Joe Harris

ISBN: 978-1-83857-679-0
CH007356US
Supplier 26, Date 0520, Print run 9826

Printed in China

CHILDREN'S ENCYCLOPEDIA OF SCIENCE EXPERIMENTS

CONTENTS

Materials

This encyclopedia reveals important ideas in science through experiments that you can perform for yourself, at home, without any special scientific equipment. In this first chapter you'll investigate materials science—the study of the chemical properties of matter. That includes matter in its various forms: Solid, liquid, and gas.

Unfolding secrets

Materials come in all shapes, sizes, states, and temperatures. When you start thinking of materials, you're thinking of the world itself. Whether you're observing an iceberg breaking off the Antarctic coast, a glass falling to the floor and smashing, or an ice cream melting and dripping down your hand, you're learning about materials and how they behave.

The experiments in the following pages will take you into a world where materials bend, break, melt, expand, contract, and sometimes behave in ways that may at first seem confusing. By the end of the chapter you'll see how everyday materials hide some real mysteries—and how mysterious objects might turn out to be familiar.

DID YOU KNOW? Materials science is a wide-ranging field, which covers physics and chemistry and ties in with several branches of engineering.

Invisible Gases

Most gases are invisible, but we can still observe some of their properties and how they behave. A relatively dense and heavy gas, for example, will sink through a lighter one, just as a heavier liquid sinks through a lighter liquid. Try this experiment on a bright, sunny day in front of a light-colored wall that faces the sun.

1

On a table by the wall, assemble baking soda, vinegar, a pitcher, a tablespoon, and a wooden spoon.

2

Pour 200 ml of vinegar into the pitcher.

3

Add 2 tablespoons of baking soda to the vinegar and stir with the wooden spoon.

4

Hold the pitcher out so that its shadow is visible on the wall behind you.

5

Slowly tip the pitcher, taking care that none of the liquid pours out.

6

You should see the shadow of the gas pouring out.

YOU WILL NEED: baking soda | vinegar | a pitcher | a tablespoon | a wooden spoon

When you mix the baking soda with vinegar in the pitcher, it triggers a chemical reaction that produces a gas called carbon dioxide. That gas is denser and heavier than air, so it can be "poured" just as a liquid could be poured.

Unlike air, the denser carbon dioxide gas casts a shadow. It's that shadow of the heavy gas that you see being poured from the pitcher.

Natural gas flows out from oil wells as oil is extracted. Unlike carbon dioxide, the dispersing gas is lighter than air, so it rises.

Natural gas is normally invisible, but it burns brightly once oil engineers disperse it by lighting it.

DID YOU KNOW? Carbon dioxide can be poured over a candle to block its air supply and extinguish the flame, which is how fire extinguishers work.

Firm Foundations

Buildings need firm foundations to prevent them from collapsing or toppling over. So, before engineers plan a building, they first need to consider what they are building on. As you'll discover in this experiment, when laying foundations it's important to think about both balance and strength.

1

Scrunch up about six sheets of paper and arrange them in a shoebox shape on the floor.

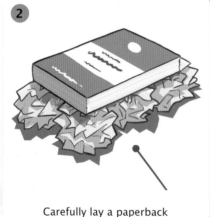

2

Carefully lay a paperback book on the scrunched up paper.

3

Add more books until the pile tips over.

4

Scrunch up another six sheets of paper and arrange them in a shoebox.

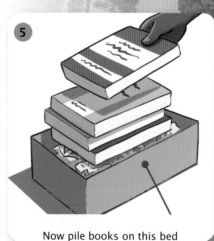

5

Now pile books on this bed of scrunched-up paper.

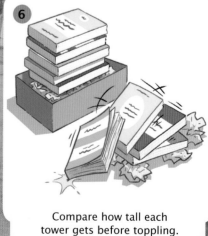

6

Compare how tall each tower gets before toppling.

YOU WILL NEED: 12 sheets of newspaper | 20 paperback books (roughly the same size) | a shoebox

Just like the first pile of books, Italy's Leaning Tower of Pisa has "foundation problems." The famous building started tilting just a few years after construction began in 1172.

The sandy soil beneath the tower isn't stable enough to support the weight evenly.

HOW DOES IT WORK?

The experiment with the books shows how effective foundations use force to support overhead structures. The scrunched-up paper under the first pile of books was forced outward by the downward pressure of gravity on the books. Without any other support, the pile became less stable, so the books toppled.

However, under the second pile of books, the sides of the shoebox acted like the walls of a deep foundation—holding the paper in place and maintaining stability. That extra stability lets more books be stacked on top of the paper.

DID YOU KNOW? An engineering rescue project in the 1990s slightly lessened the angle of the Leaning Tower of Pisa's tilt.

Metal Mysteries

We think of metals as strong, unbending construction materials. But not all metals are alike: For example, mercury is a liquid at room temperature. And even the most solid metals can surprise us. It's all due to the movement of the molecules that make them up. See for yourself with this experiment.

1. Tighten the lids of both jars so that it would be hard to unscrew them.

2. Hold one of the jars in the sink and run cold water over it.

3. Continue holding it there for 30 seconds and try to unscrew it. It will still feel stiff.

4. Repeat the steps with the second jar, this time running water that's hot (but not too hot to touch).

5. Try to unscrew its lid; you should find it much easier.

YOU WILL NEED: two identical jam jars with metal lids | hot and cold water

The steel used for roller-coaster rails is strong, but, like the lid of the jar held under hot water, it still expands when heated.

In extremely hot weather, the side-to-side movement of a heavy train can make the expanded rails bend, and roller-coasters sometimes have to be closed as a precaution.

HOW DOES IT WORK?

The experiment with the glass jars demonstrates how the metal lid expands when it is warmed. Scientists call this thermal expansion. It happens when the heated molecules in the metal begin to move farther apart. The result is that the metal gets slightly bigger.

The glass jar also expands, but much less than the metal. That means that the metal lid "outgrows" the jar and becomes a little bit looser.

DID YOU KNOW? The John Hancock Tower, a skyscraper in Boston, once lost hundreds of windows because the metal frames expanded in the heat.

Molecule Magic

The secret to shape-shifting is hidden in materials' molecules. Hard materials have molecules that are locked tightly together. But if there are more gaps between molecules, the material is more flexible. Demonstrate the magic of molecules with this amazing experiment.

1 Half–fill the bag with water, zip it shut, and hold it at the top.

2 Slowly poke a sharpened pencil through the plastic.

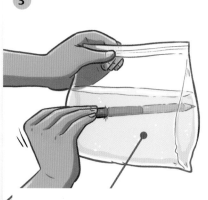

3 Continue until the pencil passes through the water and out the other side.

4 Check for drops on either side—the bag should stay dry.

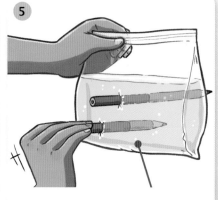

5 Continue adding pencils and observing your "magic trick."

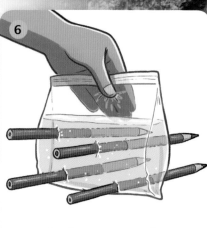

6 See how many pencils you can fit in.

YOU WILL NEED: a ziplock sandwich bag | water | sharp pencils

An octopus has a magic trick too. With no hard bones, it can squeeze its soft body through a narrow gap and regain its shape on the other side.

Its incredible ability to change shape gives an octopus an excellent means of escape.

HOW DOES IT WORK?

The magic trick on the opposite page works because the plastic sandwich bag is made up of polymers—strings of molecules that can bend and stretch and then tighten again. When you push a pencil through the bag, the hole you make is a bit like the neck-hole in your sweater. It widens to let your head through and then reshapes around your neck. Similarly, the polymer molecules ease apart as the pencil enters and then tighten around it, so there are no leaks.

DID YOU KNOW? One fully grown octopus that weighed 600 pounds was once able to squeeze through a hole the size of a large coin.

Acid Power

Acids are chemicals that react with other substances—sometimes with dramatic results. Strong acids break things down quickly, like the acid in our stomachs, helping us to digest food. Weaker acids act more slowly. You can see the power of an acid in this experiment with vinegar and a leftover chicken bone.

1. Rinse and dry a chicken bone. A drumstick about as long as your finger is ideal for this experiment.

2. Place the bone in a glass jar and cover it with vinegar.

3. Screw the lid back on the jar and leave it for two to three days.

4. Pour the vinegar out and rinse the bone.

5. Dry the bone with the paper towel and feel it wiggle.

6. It will look and feel like rubber.

YOU WILL NEED: a chicken bone | vinegar | a jar with a lid

Chicken bones, like human bones, get their hardness from calcium carbonate and other minerals. Vinegar contains acetic acid. When left to soak for a few days, the vinegar slowly breaks down calcium carbonate in the bone and eventually dissolves the calcium.

The bone loses its hardness but keeps its shape. The bendy bone is flexible because collagen, a rubbery protein, remains after the reaction with the acid.

Mild acids can form in the air when chemicals are emitted from factory chimneys. They mix with rainwater to make acid rain.

Like the vinegar reacting with the bone, acid rain damages trees and plants, gradually turning many forests into graveyards of dead or dying trees.

DID YOU KNOW? Acid rain also eats away at buildings and monuments, making it impossible to recognize the faces of many statues.

Quirky Colloids

Atoms are the basic building blocks for all matter. Materials are made up of molecules—atoms that group together through chemical attraction. Chemistry also holds the molecules together in most substances. A colloid is a bit different: It's a mixture of substances that aren't held together chemically. The result can be truly quirky, as you will see in this experiment.

1 Put four tablespoons of cornstarch in the mixing bowl, spreading it evenly across the bottom of the bowl.

2 Fill the cup with cold water from the faucet and keep it to hand.

3 Dip the teaspoon in the cup and add about spoonful of water to the cornstarch.

4 Stir the cornstarch-water mixture thoroughly with the fork.

5 Repeat several times, checking the mixture with your finger.

6 The mixture should now be runny if left alone, but firm when poked.

YOU WILL NEED: a medium mixing bowl | cornstarch | a tablespoon | a cup | water | a teaspoon | a fork

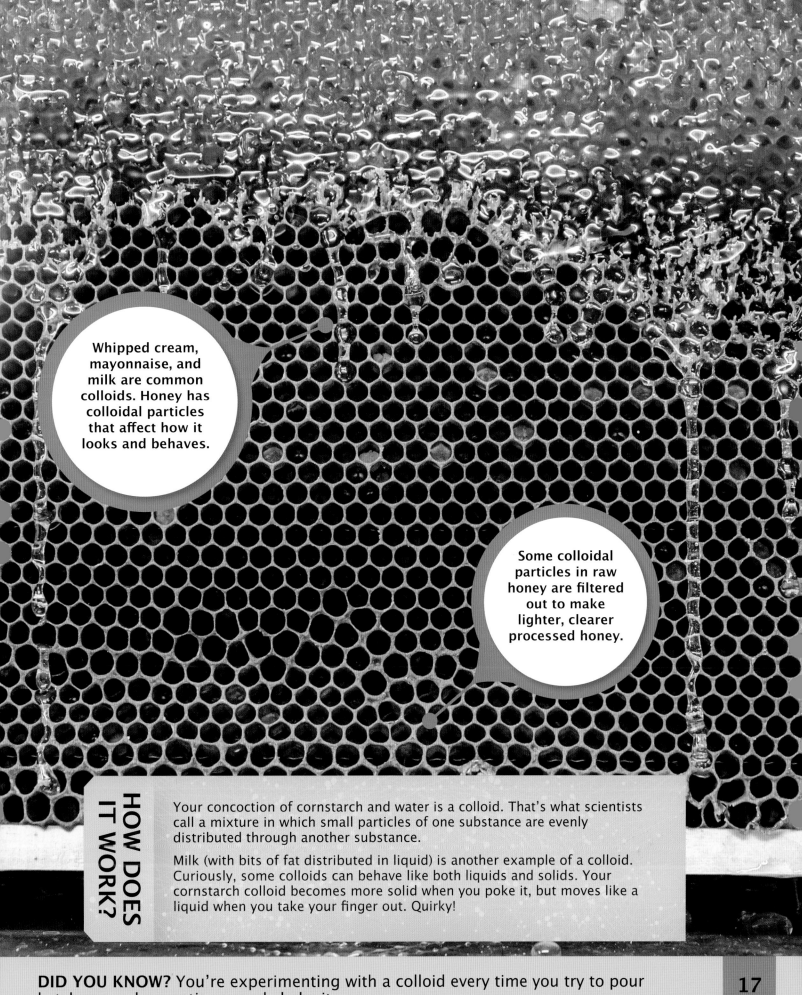

Whipped cream, mayonnaise, and milk are common colloids. Honey has colloidal particles that affect how it looks and behaves.

Some colloidal particles in raw honey are filtered out to make lighter, clearer processed honey.

HOW DOES IT WORK?

Your concoction of cornstarch and water is a colloid. That's what scientists call a mixture in which small particles of one substance are evenly distributed through another substance.

Milk (with bits of fat distributed in liquid) is another example of a colloid. Curiously, some colloids can behave like both liquids and solids. Your cornstarch colloid becomes more solid when you poke it, but moves like a liquid when you take your finger out. Quirky!

DID YOU KNOW? You're experimenting with a colloid every time you try to pour ketchup—or lose patience and shake it.

Sticky Chemicals

Chemistry is all about attraction—links between positive protons and negative electrons inside atoms, or between differently charged atoms. On a larger scale, some molecules stick to similar ones (that's cohesion), while others attract different ones—adhesion. This experiment shows both types of attraction.

1
Tie the yarn to the handle of the pitcher using a double knot.

2
Fill the pitcher about two-thirds with water.

3
Plunge the yarn into the water until it's completely submerged.

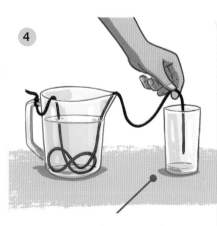

4
Put the free (not tied) end of the yarn in the drinking glass.

5
Raise the pitcher and pour very slowly, keeping the yarn taut.

6
The water will pour down the yarn into the glass.

YOU WILL NEED: 3ft of yarn | a small pitcher | a glass | another pitcher filled with water

Adhesion snares the prey in a spiderweb. An insect literally gets stuck to the surface of the web.

Spiders don't get stuck in their webs because they walk on strands that aren't sticky, and their legs have a nonstick chemical coating.

HOW DOES IT WORK?

The water and yarn experiment demonstrates two important properties of water—it is both cohesive and adhesive. Its molecules are attracted to other water molecules and also to different molecules.

Adhesion causes the water to stick to the different molecules in the yarn. Cohesion causes the water molecules to stick together. So, as water flows down the string it drags more water down with it. And it doesn't drip along the way.

DID YOU KNOW? A spiderweb is so effective not just thanks to its adhesive properties—it's also because the strands are five times stronger than steel.

Changing States

Cooking is a domestic science and this experiment helps you understand why—heating and cooling a material causes the particles to act differently, changing its state. Here, the chocolate changes from a solid to a liquid state and back again. Make sure to ask an adult to help with the boiling water.

1. Rinse the rose leaves and dry them with a paper towel. Pat them lightly as they rest on a paper towel.

2. Half-fill the saucepan with water and ask an adult to warm it.

3. Break up the chocolate into small pieces and put them in the mixing bowl.

4. Ask the adult to put the bowl on top of the pan. When it's melted, ask the adult to give you the bowl.

5. Use the melted chocolate to "paint" the rose leaves and leave them to cool.

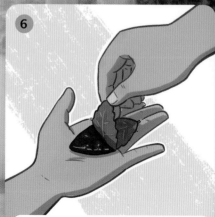

6. Now, remove the leaves to reveal an imprinted leaf pattern.

YOU WILL NEED: 5 rose leaves | paper towel | water | a saucepan | a mixing bowl | a bar of chocolate | a clean paintbrush

Materials have different freezing points. Chocolate is solid at room temperature, but water is a liquid. Here, the water dripping from a warm roof freezes in the sub-freezing air at the edge, creating solid icicles.

The weak winter sun isn't warm enough to melt the icicles, so they remain hanging in their frozen, solid state.

HOW DOES IT WORK?

In the cooking experiment, the molecules inside the chocolate are tightly packed, keeping it solid at room temperature. As the chocolate warms, those molecules begin to move more quickly and farther apart. When the chocolate melts, it changes into a liquid state. This process is used to make chocolate into shapes, by pouring it into moulds, where it sets into bars, buttons, and even figures.

DID YOU KNOW? Chocolate is the only edible substance to melt around 90°F, just below human body temperature—that's why it melts in your mouth.

Layering on Strength

Layered (laminated) materials are often sturdier than a single layer of the same thickness. Many materials, such as wood, have strengthening fibers or grains. Laminates often also alternate layers in different directions, providing extra strength. This impressive experiment demonstrates the effect. Find an adult to help with this one.

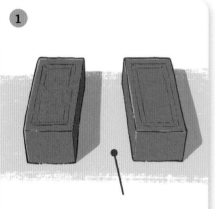

1 Put the bricks on a floor or counter—slightly closer to each other than the length of a Popsicle stick.

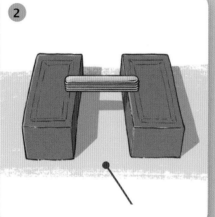

2 Pile five sticks to make a bridge between the bricks.

3 Ask an adult to break them with a hammer blow. The sticks should go flying but not break.

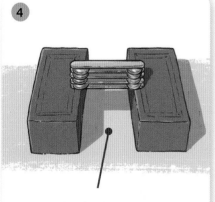

4 Pile them again but add a coin at each end of each level.

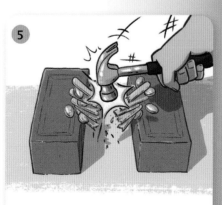

5 Ask the adult to try again—most sticks should break.

YOU WILL NEED: two bricks | 10 Popsicle sticks | eight identical coins | a hammer

A fast-moving karate kick can pack enough hammer-like force to break wood.

Lighter wood, with air pockets acting as spacers, is easier to break with a kick or hammerblow.

HOW DOES IT WORK?

This demonstration is all down to laminates, or layers. The first "bridge" withstood the hammerblow because it behaved like one material, but with five layers. The same number of sticks piled up with coin "spacers" was easier to break, because the hammer hit each one separately. It takes less force to break one stick than five stuck together.

Some karate demonstrations also use spacers between piles of boards—it would be much harder to chop them without those spacers.

DID YOU KNOW? Laminated glass is much stronger than ordinary glass—which is why it's used in car windows.

Forces

Scientists describe a force as strength or energy to cause or change movement. When someone gives you a push on your bike, they're applying force. You might then brake, applying the force of friction, to slow down to prevent falling, which is caused by another force—gravity.

Strength and Energy

Think of some of the more familiar forces that involve pushing or pulling—picking up a heavy shopping bag, being pulled by a lively dog on a leash, or pushing a lawn mower in your backyard. They're all examples of forces at work, and it's easy to see or feel their effects. With a bit of exploring, and experiments, you can discover some fascinating secrets about forces.

For example, did you know that water and even air can provide a powerful force? Or that you can change a force with tricks of time or space? The following pages will help you see forces can cause or change movement in some surprising ways.

Tunnels of Air

Gases can generate or change powerful forces. But you can see some of those forces in action with a familiar gas that's always around you—air. This simple experiment with an air current from a blow-dryer and a table tennis ball can help demonstrate how huge aircraft can fly without falling out of the sky.

1 Turn the blow-dryer to the coolest level. This experiment depends on moving air, not heat.

2 Point the blow-dryer up, holding the ball in your other hand and turn it on.

3 Slowly move the ball toward the upward-flowing air, approaching the dryer from above.

4 Release the ball when you feel it begin to move in your hand.

5 The ball will float just where you let it go.

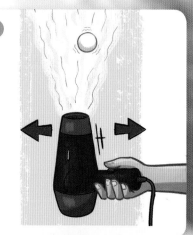

6 See what happens if you move the blow-dryer from side to side.

YOU WILL NEED: a blow-dryer (ask permission before you borrow it) | a table tennis ball

Warming air rises, like a tunnel of air rushing from the blow-dryer. We call the upward currents, "thermals." An eagle uses thermals to glide for long periods.

Broad wings catch as much wind as possible.

HOW DOES IT WORK?

The table tennis ball experiment depends on Bernoulli's principle, which states that a gas exerts less pressure (pushes less hard) as it moves faster. Air presses in every direction, so the air rushing out of the blow-dryer is like a tunnel of weak pressure surrounded by higher pressure.

The rushing air pushes up the table tennis ball, but farther away is air that is still, and this pushes on the current of moving air. Even if you tilt the blow-dryer, the ball will still float, held inside its "tunnel" by the still air around it.

DID YOU KNOW? Aircraft designers study birds' wings to find out how to get the most lift (upward force) possible.

Air Force

Air and other gases do more than lift objects or blow them about. They can gain enormous strength—providing extra force—as their pressure increases. An ordinary balloon builds up pressure as it is blown up, because more and more gas (air) is being pushed into a limited space (the shape of the balloon). Keep on blowing and the increasing pressure will burst the balloon … but that same increasing pressure can also be put to work, as this experiment shows.

1
Set the pitchers side by side on a counter or table where you'll be experimenting.

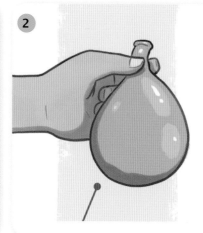

2
Blow up one balloon about one-quarter full and pinch it to stop the air escaping.

3
Keeping the balloon pinched, lower it carefully to the bottom of the smaller measuring pitcher.

4
Hold the pitcher firmly and continue inflating the balloon until it becomes difficult.

5
Keeping the balloon pinched, pick up the pitcher.

6
Now repeat steps 2-5 with the bigger pitcher and see how what happens.

YOU WILL NEED: a small plastic pitcher | a big plastic pitcher | 2 balloons

HOW DOES IT WORK?

Even the most ordinary, everyday action uses force. When you pick up a pitcher, your fingers are exerting force inward (gripping the handle). Blowing up the balloon creates an outward force that allows the balloon to "grip" the inside of the pitcher.

For the second balloon and the bigger pitcher, you'll need to blow more, to fill a bigger space with air. But blowing more increases the pressure further, adding enough force to lift the extra weight.

Construction vehicles weigh several tons and carry equally heavy loads, all putting force on the wheels.

Air pressure gives the balloon-like tires the strength to support the vehicle as well as its weighty load.

DID YOU KNOW? An inflated balloon shrinks in deep water because the water pressure is stronger than the air pressure inside.

The Skin of Water

If we throw a coin into a fountain or a stone into a lake, they sink. But a closer look at the calm surface of water shows something remarkable. Its chemical properties create surface tension. This enables water to resist an outside force (gravity), so that some objects you'd expect to sink, don't. You can show how surface tension acts like a skin with this magic, floating-needle trick.

1

Fill the clear drinking glass nearly to the top with water. Cold water is fine.

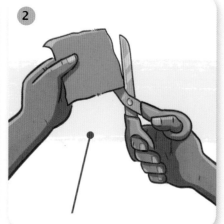

2

Cut the tissue paper into a square, each side about as long as the needle.

3

Make sure that the water is still and lay the tissue on the water's surface.

4

Carefully lay the needle on the tissue.

5

Watch the tissue sink to the bottom of the glass.

6

The needle should stay resting on the surface of the water.

YOU WILL NEED: a glass | water | tissue paper | a needle | scissors

HOW DOES IT WORK?

Water is made up of molecules (hydrogen and oxygen atoms bonded together). The water molecules stick to each other through cohesion, and this happens more strongly where they meet air. This sticking together creates surface tension, like a thin skin on the surface of the water.

In your experiment, the tissue paper is porous, which means that water is able to pass through. When it has absorbed enough water, it sinks. The metal needle doesn't absorb water, so it is held up by the "skin."

Some insects use surface tension to walk across water, like this water boatman.

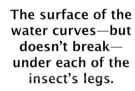

The surface of the water curves—but doesn't break— under each of the insect's legs.

DID YOU KNOW? Surface tension also explains the bulge that can be seen on the still surface of water in a glass.

Balancing Act

An object balances when its overall mass is the same either side of an imaginary balancing point. This point is its center of mass. We can imagine that the downward force of gravity is concentrated on that point—like the midpoint of a seesaw. If the mass is unevenly distributed, then that point won't be in the measured middle of the object. You can show how uneven weight affects balance with this magic trick.

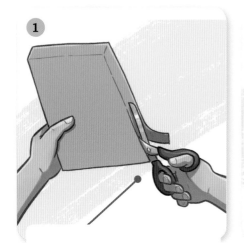

1

Use the scissors to cut the overhanging "lip" around the shoebox lid.

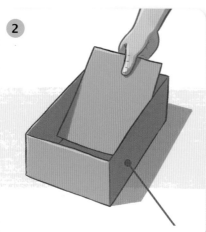

2

Check that the lid can become a false bottom later.

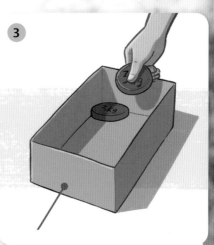

3

Add the weights to the box, tucked closely against one end of the shoebox.

4

Place the false bottom in the shoebox again, so that the weights are hidden.

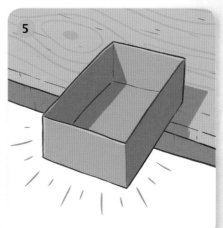

5

Slide the box halfway over a table-edge, with the weights in the end on the table—it won't fall off.

A tightrope walker keeps his center of mass directly over the tightrope, so gravity acts evenly and he doesn't fall to one side.

YOU WILL NEED: a shoebox | scissors | kitchen weights

HOW DOES IT WORK?

Think about how you stretch your arms out when walk in a very straight line. You might not have realized it, but you're constantly adjusting your center of mass. That's the point where your mass is balanced—with the same amount either side. The shoebox experiment works because the kitchen weights have more mass than the cardboard, so the box can jut out well past the end of the table without falling. Gravity holds the heavier (more massive) end on the table.

Stretching out or pulling back his arms enables the tightrope walker to adjust his center of mass.

DID YOU KNOW? People sometimes refer to center of mass as "center of gravity" because it suggests avoiding falls.

Staying Afloat

Two forces, working in opposite directions, determine whether an object (or person) will float or sink in water. Gravity pushes the object downward, while buoyancy pushes it up. The shape of the object helps determine whether it is buoyant enough to float, which explains why a pebble sinks, but a massive ship can float. This experiment uses simple modeling clay to show that the buoyancy of an object is affected by its shape.

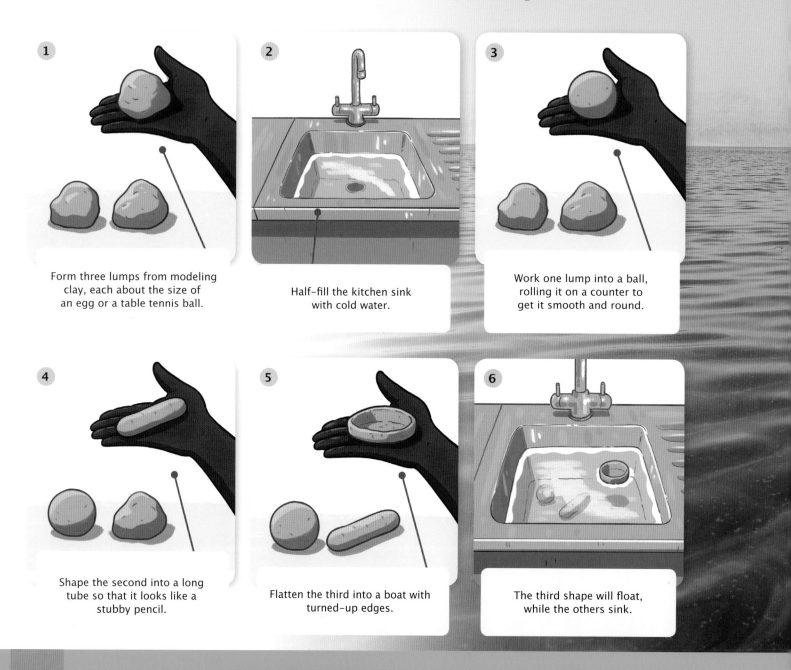

1. Form three lumps from modeling clay, each about the size of an egg or a table tennis ball.

2. Half-fill the kitchen sink with cold water.

3. Work one lump into a ball, rolling it on a counter to get it smooth and round.

4. Shape the second into a long tube so that it looks like a stubby pencil.

5. Flatten the third into a boat with turned-up edges.

6. The third shape will float, while the others sink.

YOU WILL NEED: modeling clay | sink filled with water

The first two modeling clay shapes sink quickly. The third—which most resembles a boat—will float. That's because of the upward-pushing force called buoyancy.

Whether something floats depends on how much water it displaces (pushes aside) as it rests on the surface. It will float if the force of gravity on that displaced water is greater than the force of gravity on the object itself. The modeling clay boat displaces more water than the other two shapes, allowing it to float.

The salt content of water is another thing that affects buoyancy. Things float more easily in very salty water—like the Dead Sea, a lake which is nine times saltier than the sea.

Our body weight is lighter than the density of salt water, so we can float in the sea when we might sink in a freshwater lake.

DID YOU KNOW? Huge, heavy ships can still float because their large size displaces lots of water.

Easing the Pressure

Someone wearing high-heel shoes will leave a deeper footprint in soft soil than an elephant walking along the same path. How can that be, if the elephant is 100 times heavier than the person in heels? It's all because of how forces can be changed by spreading them over a greater surface area, to ease the pressure. To prove it, this experiment goes with a bang!

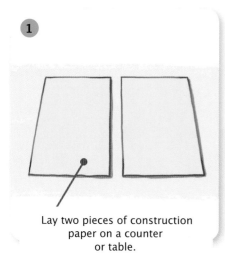

1 Lay two pieces of construction paper on a counter or table.

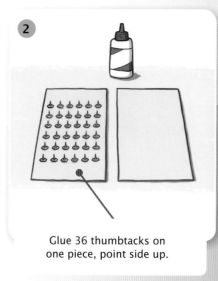

2 Glue 36 thumbtacks on one piece, point side up.

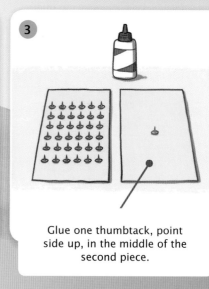

3 Glue one thumbtack, point side up, in the middle of the second piece.

4 Inflate and tie two balloons while the glue dries.

5 Press one balloon against the single tack: It will pop.

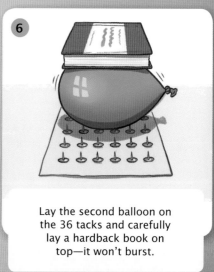

6 Lay the second balloon on the 36 tacks and carefully lay a hardback book on top—it won't burst.

YOU WILL NEED: construction paper | a glue | thumbtacks | 2 balloons | a hardback book

The balloon pops because its downward force is concentrated in one point: The point of the single drawing pin. When when that same force is spread across the 36 tacks it can't pop the balloon.

Scientists define pressure as "force over area." In other words, a small area of contact (the single tack) is the focus of all of your downward force. That same force—or even a larger one from the weight of the book—spreads the pressure evenly when the area of contact (lots of tacks) covers a wider area.

Camels have special adaptations to their feet which enable them to walk long distances on soft sand.

The camel's toes spread out and flatten as it walks. This increases the surface area of the foot so the camel doesn't sink into the sand, despite its weight.

DID YOU KNOW? Daring circus performers use the same science to lie safely on a bed of nails.

All in a Spin

Momentum is defined as an object's mass multiplied by its velocity (speed). Objects moving in a straight line have linear momentum. A spinning object, though, has angular momentum. An object's angular momentum also takes into account its distance from an axis. This neat experiment demonstrates how adding width helps an object to maintain a controlled spin.

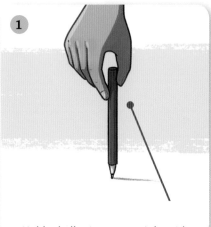

1

Hold a ballpoint pen upright with its tip on a smooth flat surface like a table top or floor.

2

Twist it with your fingers: It will fall over almost immediately.

As she draws her arms closer, she begins to spin faster—and can take off and jump into the air.

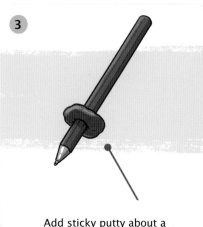

3

Add sticky putty about a thumb's width above the point.

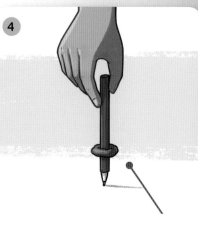

4

Try spinning the pen carefully.

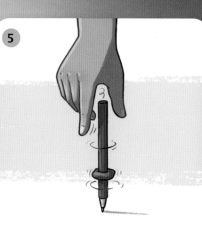

5

It will stay upright once you let go.

YOU WILL NEED: a ball-point pen | sticky putty

Spinning objects move faster but with less control if their width gets smaller, all due to angular momentum. This explains why the (wider) pen with the putty stayed upright when it was spun.

Angular momentum also enables a figure skater to spin faster as she draws her arms closer to her body.

A skater's fast spin takes real concentration and training to ensure her body is in the exact position at each step.

Like your pen spinning on its tip, the skater's weight is concentrated on the tips of her skates as she spins.

DID YOU KNOW? Wider wheels, like full-sized bike wheels, are more stable than smaller wheels because of angular momentum.

Marvelous Momentum

Momentum always involves force, as well as mass and velocity (speed and direction). The combined momentum of two objects is conserved after they collide. So, the total momentum remains the same, but it can be transferred from one object to another. Try this easy experiment to show conservation of momentum in action.

1

Hold a basketball or volleyball at arm's length and drop it on to a hard surface outside.

2

Note how high the basketball bounces.

3

Do the same with a tennis ball.

4

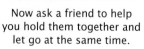

Now ask a friend to help you hold them together and let go at the same time.

5

The tennis ball will bounce much higher than either ball did before.

YOU WILL NEED: a basketball/volleyball | a tennis ball | a volunteer

This experiment demonstrates conservation of momentum. That simply means that when two objects collide, their combined momentum remains the same. However, some of the momentum might be lost from one object (the basketball in this case) and transferred to another (the tennis ball). So when the balls are dropped together—and collide—the tennis ball receives extra momentum that sends it sky-high.

Carnival rides help turn conservation of momentum into boundless fun.

"Bumper cars" offer constant demonstrations of this effect as they collide and bounce off one another.

DID YOU KNOW? Astronauts in the International Space Station have demonstrated conservation of momentum, with tennis balls floating in the gravity-free atmosphere.

Resistant Friction

We encounter friction all around us every day. It's the force that acts between two objects that are in contact, and it resists movement. As with other forces, a small amount goes unnoticed. But if it builds, then it's hard to ignore. Even the pages of books can be locked together using no more than the force of friction, as this experiment shows.

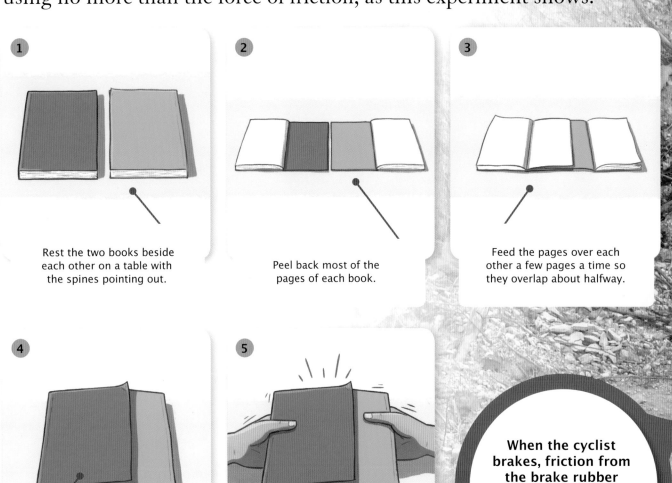

1 Rest the two books beside each other on a table with the spines pointing out.

2 Peel back most of the pages of each book.

3 Feed the pages over each other a few pages a time so they overlap about halfway.

4 Continue in this way until you reach the front.

5 Ask a friend to pull the books apart—they will be stuck.

When the cyclist brakes, friction from the brake rubber resists the wheel's rotation and slows the bike down.

YOU WILL NEED: 2 paperback books

The books in your experiment stick together due to the force of friction, which resists the movement of the pages sliding against each other.

Each overlay of pages creates a small amount of friction, which you can feel if you slide the pages back and forth. Every overlay adds another small bit of force, then another, and so on. Eventually there is such a build-up of friction that the books are locked together.

Racing sports rely on friction to safely control speed. Some turns on hillside trails are too tight for BMX racers to take fast—they must slow down.

DID YOU KNOW? One version of this experiment was done with enormous books—and even trucks couldn't pull them apart.

Momentum in Time

An object's momentum changes when it collides with something, and the force this produces depends on how long the collision takes. A longer period of time spreads out the change in momentum, just as an airbag protects passengers by slowing their forward movement in a crash. The egg in this experiment shouldn't break, thanks to the flexible sheet absorbing its impact—but it's best to do it outside just in case.

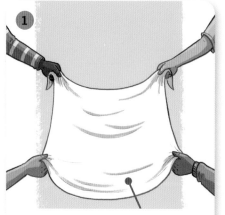

Ask three volunteers to help you loosely hold a tablecloth flat, so that it forms a trough.

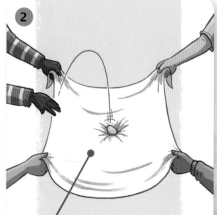

Throw an egg directly at the middle of the cloth.

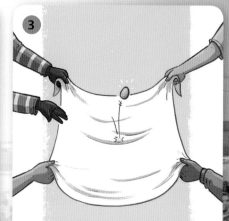

The egg won't break as it hits the cloth as its impact is absorbed.

HOW DOES IT WORK?

Momentum, an object's mass and velocity (speed), is affected by how long a collision takes. If you threw an egg at a wall it would splat—because the hard wall does not absorb the force of the impact, so the egg comes to an instant stop.

Here, the springy sheet gives way a little. It absorbs the impact, meaning that the force is shared out for a longer period of time, and the egg is protected from breaking.

YOU WILL NEED: an old bedsheet or tablecloth (ask before using it) | an egg | 3 volunteers

Like the egg thrown at the tablecloth, a person tossed on a blanket is protected because the flexible blanket gives way, making sure it's a soft landing.

Blanket tossing is a traditional sport of the Inuit and other native peoples in Alaska.

DID YOU KNOW? A tennis drop shot and trapping a pass in soccer are examples of controlling momentum and time.

45

Light and Sound

We use two of our senses—sight and hearing—to help us make sense of our surroundings. Some of the most interesting experiments involve light and sound. They both travel through space in waves, and understanding this wave motion unlocks some of the secrets of these forms of energy.

Solving mysteries

Scientists can measure the distance between these waves (or wavelength) as well as how many times they vibrate in a single second (their frequency). Whatever we see or hear are the results of those energy wavelengths and frequencies, making things change color or pitch.

Both sound and light waves can "bend" or be reflected along the way as they hit or pass through some materials. Those changed paths can also lead to light and sound becoming focused, making them particularly powerful within a relatively small area. What we see or hear also depends on whether the source of the light or sound is heading toward or away from us. These distortions can be confusing, making people question the evidence of their senses. The following experiments aim to answer those questions while prompting you to think of questions of your own.

DID YOU KNOW? Light travels around 900,000 times faster than sound, which is why we see lightning before we hear thunder.

The Sound of Music

Even if we don't realize it, we use science—and mathematics—to appreciate our best-loved songs and melodies. You can even demonstrate this connection between science and music with an easy experiment to create sound waves, complete with a makeshift musical instrument, at home.

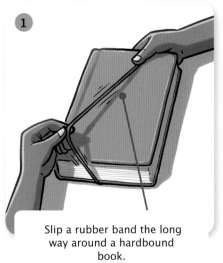

1 Slip a rubber band the long way around a hardbound book.

2 Slide the two pencils under the loop near end of the book.

> Like the strings on musical instruments, vocal cords in our throat vibrate to make different sounds.

3 Pluck the band (now slightly raised) and listen to the musical note.

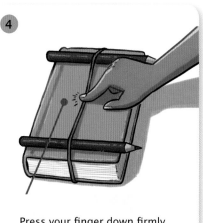
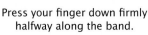

4 Press your finger down firmly halfway along the band.

5 Pluck again and listen to the different tone.

YOU WILL NEED: a hardback book | a rubber band | 2 pencils

A microphone amplifies a singer's voice. It makes it sound stronger, but it doesn't change the notes that she sings.

HOW DOES IT WORK?

The rubber band in your experiment vibrates like a guitar string. When you shorten the string by half its length (Step 4) and pluck the band either side, it sounds like the same note, but higher. In fact, it's an octave higher. If you called the first note "Do," and then sang up the scale, through "Re," "Mi," and so on, the second note would be a higher "Do." The sound waves vibrate twice as fast (we hear it as one octave higher) when the band is half is long.

DID YOU KNOW? The strings of a harp have different lengths, so that each plays a different note.

Light Reflections

When we see ourselves reflected in a mirror, it's because of the way that light behaves. Visible light (which the human eye can see) extends over a range of colors: Red, orange, yellow, green, blue, indigo, and violet. All of them combine to create white light. Sometimes only one color reflects off an object, and that gives the object its hue. You can see for yourself with this simple and quick experiment—which you can do anywhere at home.

1

Try this in a darkened room—not necessarily pitch-dark, but with lights out or curtains drawn.

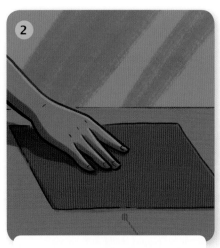

2

Lay the construction paper on a table.

3

Stand slightly away from the table and shine the flashlight down on the paper.

4

Have a friend hold some white paper beyond the table, where the beam will be reflected.

5

The light on the paper will show the card's color.

YOU WILL NEED: colored construction paper | a flashlight | a volunteer | white paper

Just as we see the color of the paper, we see the tree as green because that's the only color that is reflected.

The still water is like a mirror, reflecting every tint of color in the landscape.

HOW DOES IT WORK?

Light reflected (bouncing off) a mirror shows a "mirror image" of us—including all the colors. But light usually gets absorbed by objects it hits, except for certain colors that get reflected. So when we see a red apple, it's because red is reflected. The other shades in the light have been absorbed.

The same thing happens when the light is shone down on the card and you see it reflect its color onto the white paper.

DID YOU KNOW? Write something backward and put it up to a mirror: The reflection will be the right way around.

Super Sounds

The strength of moving sound waves changes after meeting another object. If the sound waves reflected from the meeting point reflect back at the same frequency, the sound can actually strengthen. And reflecting off a curved surface can focus that strengthened sound. Hear such super sounds for yourself in this clever experiment.

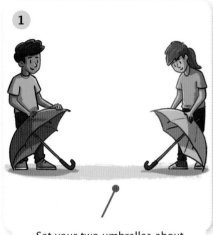

1

Set your two umbrellas about 20ft apart with their handles pointing at each other.

2

Tie the watch to one handle, about 15 inches up from the base.

3

Lie by the other umbrella, with your ear also about 15 inches up from the base.

4

Listen—you should hear the watch ticking clearly.

YOU WILL NEED: 2 umbrellas | an analogue wristwatch | string | a volunteer

The ticking watch sends out sound waves in a steady pattern, or frequency. Just about every material also has what's called a "natural frequency." If a sound with a similar frequency hits that material, it will become amplified (strengthened). This process is called resonance.

In your experiment, the ticking sound hits the inside of one umbrella and is amplified. Then the curved shape focuses that louder sound and sends it off to the other umbrella.

Think of each "tick" from the watch as being like a raindrop hitting a puddle.

The sound waves travel outward, just as the raindrop sends out waves in every direction in the puddle.

DID YOU KNOW? Sound resonance can also break glasses by causing vibrations that increase until the brittle glass shatters.

Doppler Effect

Listen to the whine of a racing car. It seems to get lower as the car moves away from you, even though you know that it's really the same. This is an example of the Doppler Effect, which explains how sound waves widen as the sound source speeds away from you—and become shorter as that same source speeds closer to you. Demonstrate the Doppler Effect to your friends in this fun experiment.

1 Fit a funnel into one end of 7ft length of rubber hose. It should be snug.

2 Fit some modeling clay around it to seal it in place.

3 Hold a whistle secure by clamping your lips around it.

4 Cover your mouth (including the whistle) with the funnel and keep holding it to your mouth.

5 Swing the hose while blowing the whistle.

6 Have a friend listen to the sound as it seems to swing around.

YOU WILL NEED: funnel | 7ft rubber hose | modeling clay | a whistle | a volunteer

Your friend will hear the pitch go up and down as the hose moves toward them and away. It's caused by the Doppler Effect. Remember how sound waves spread out from the source of a sound like the ripples in the puddle? Well, as the hose moves toward the listener, the waves bunch together, decreasing the wavelength, so the sound has a higher pitch. As the hose moves farther away, the waves spread out, increasing the wavelength, making it sound lower to you than it actually is.

Racing cars are excellent examples of the Doppler Effect in action. Spectators hear a changing pitch as the cars speed by.

But like when you swing the hose, the driver hears the same sound all the while they're driving.

DID YOU KNOW? The Doppler Effect also works with light, which becomes redder as it moves away from us—astrophysicists use this to measure the velocity of stars.

How to Bend Light

Light will travel in a straight path—like the Sun's light reaching Earth—unless it hits something to change that path. One result is reflection, or bouncing off an object. But other, stranger, effects can occur as light passes through some substances. The light can then change direction, or refract, as it continues on its path. You'll need a darkened room to show off your light-bending skill in this experiment.

1

Cut a slit about 0.2in wide and 2in high in a narrow end of the shoebox.

2

Fill the bottle with water and screw the cap on.

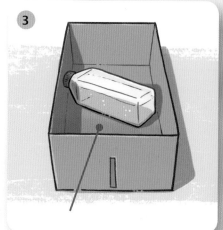

3

Angle the bottle on its side in the shoebox.

4

Draw curtains or turn off lights to darken the room.

5

Shine a flashlight through the slot.

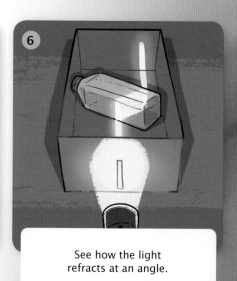

6

See how the light refracts at an angle.

YOU WILL NEED: a cardboard box | scissors | a clear water bottle with flat sides | water | a flashlight

Here's some dramatic evidence that light can bend (or refract) as it travels. Whether it does—and by how much—depends on the material that it passes through. This experiment shows how the beam of light is redirected, or refracted, as it passes through the water in the bottle.

By keeping the room dark, and the beam of the flashlight below the top of the shoebox, you make that bending path much easier to see.

The water in the bottle acts like a prism, an angled piece of clear material that refracts light.

A prism can also break down light into its different colors, just like in a rainbow.

DID YOU KNOW? Refraction will seem to "split" a spoon that's resting in a clear glass of water.

Good Vibrations

Each sound wave is created by a single vibration. And it's the rate at which those vibrations take place—their frequency—that determines the pitch of the sound we hear. This experiment is an excellent way to make that connection between vibrations and sound—with the surface of the balloon vibrating just as a vibrating guitar string produces a sound.

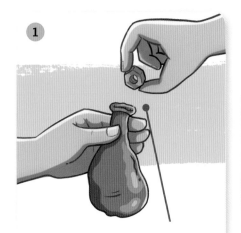

1

Feed the nut through the mouth of the balloon, shaking it so that the nut falls inside the balloon.

2

Blow the balloon up and tie it with the nut inside.

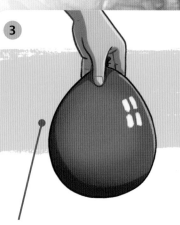

3

Hold the balloon with the palm of your hand over the knotted end.

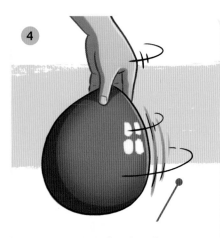

4

Move your hand as if you were stirring a spoon.

5

Soon the balloon will make an eerie whining sound.

6

Spin the balloon slower and the tone is lower.

YOU WILL NEED: a balloon | a 6-sided nut

We hear the balloon's high-pitched whine, but some sound frequencies, like bat squeaks, are too high for most humans to hear.

Bats can bounce high-frequency sounds off objects to judge distances by the echoes of those sounds.

HOW DOES IT WORK?

Two things are at work in the balloon experiment. First, each corner of the metal nut bounces against the inside of the balloon as it spins. Each bounce makes a vibration, and these vibrations begin to make a hum as the nut spins more quickly.

Second, as you spin the balloon faster and faster, the higher "bounce" frequency (the increasing number of nut bounces each second) also makes the tone of the sound higher.

DID YOU KNOW? Submarines use a similar technique to bats as they test for ocean depths.

Sharp Hearing

Sound waves become weaker as they travel away from a source. That's why you might see someone waving from across a valley but can't hear them—even if they're shouting. Our brains can cleverly judge the distance to the source of a sound, but they need to use both ears to get an accurate "reading". You can try this yourself, by judging sounds from testing distances: 5ft, 15ft, 30ft, and 35ft.

1

Find somewhere without a lot of background noise and some space—like a park.

2

Agree on a "listening point" and mark those distances.

3

A listener puts on a mask and covers an ear.

4

Shut a book loudly and ask them to guess the distance to where they think you're standing.

5

Test at several distances and with more volunteers.

6

Now have the volunteers listen with both ears.

YOU WILL NEED: a tape measure | some chalk or masking tape | volunteers | an eye mask | a book

An owl's dishlike face acts like a satellite dish to direct sounds to ears on each side.

Owls have very sharp hearing. When an owl listens, it turns its flexible head to aim both ears and pinpoint the sound source.

HOW DOES IT WORK?

When you hear the thwack of the book, your brain operates like a super-fast, super-powerful computer. It knows how long it takes sounds to reach you, and it also knows that sounds get a little fainter as they travel. So it works out the tiny difference in time and volume between the sounds reaching each ear.

Knowing those two answers lets your brain calculate the distance to the source of the sound.

DID YOU KNOW? One of an owl's ears is higher than the other, so it can judge the height of sound sources.

A Trick of the Light

You've seen how light can change direction, or refract, at an angle as it passes through some substances. But the curving path of light in this baffling experiment suggests a real bend. Concentrate on the light in the flowing water and try to suggest another explanation (that doesn't involve curving light). You'll need to find a room that can be darkened, and where it's OK to get the floor wet—and an adult to help.

1 Round up your adult to help and check that the room can be made dark.

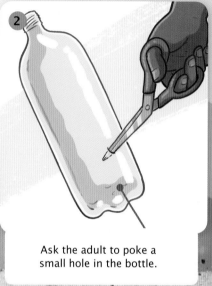

2 Ask the adult to poke a small hole in the bottle.

3 Plug the hole with your finger and fill the bottle with water.

4 Place the bottle near the edge of the counter, with the hole (still plugged) pointing out.

5 Lights off! Have a friend shine a flashlight into the bottle.

6 Remove your finger—water will stream out and the light will follow its curve.

YOU WILL NEED: a plastic water bottle (empty) | scissors | water | a plastic container | a flashlight

HOW DOES IT WORK?

Light rays travel in straight lines. The baffling bend you see in this experiment is down to reflection. Some of the light reflects off the inside of the flow of water, as if in a mirrored tunnel. That means that it follows the curve of the water—right down to the floor.

Scientists and engineers have tapped the same reflective properties to develop cables (some as narrow as a human hair) that enable light to travel long distances for high-speed internet connections and other forms of communication.

Like the water flowing from your bottle, hot air rising from the desert distorts light passing through it.

The result is a trick of light called a mirage—the distorted light looks like water.

DID YOU KNOW? Fiber-optic cables are reflective on the inside, so that light can travel through them easily.

Clever Lenses

Light behaves differently as it travels from one material to another. Light traveling through air refracts, or bends, when it passes into a clear, curved material (such as a lens). The light rays that had been parallel up to that point are focused inward. Eventually the rays meet—and cross paths—at the focal point. This experiment is an impressive demonstration of what happens when light reaches, and passes beyond, the focal point.

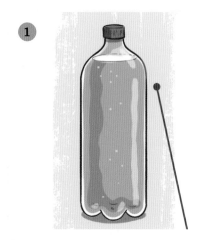

1

Fill the bottle with water and place it on the table.

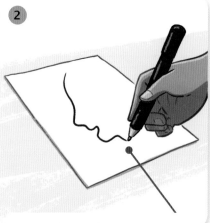

2

Draw the profile of a face on your construction paper.

3

Ask your friends to say whether face is looking left or right.

4

Now slide the construction paper behind the bottle.

5

Watch as the face flips around.

YOU WILL NEED: a tall clear bottle | construction paper | a marker pen | water | volunteers

The image reverses because, as light passes through the curved front of the bottle, it refracts (bends) toward the center. Light rays traveling through the water meet at a place called the focal point and then diverge outward again. But the light waves have crossed each other's path, reversing the image. Light refracts when it passes into a substance where it changes speed. The first light rays to reach the water bottle slow to 140,000 miles per second. Others carry on at top speed until they enter the water. That difference in speed causes the light to refract at an angle.

Like your water bottle, the glistening drops of dew on a leaf act as lenses, affecting the way we see images.

The image of the flower beyond has been reversed vertically by the lens.

DID YOU KNOW? Images passing through the lens of our eye are reversed, appearing upside-down on the retina at the back.

Heat and Cold

Changes in temperature go to the heart of how all matter behaves—from the atomic level right up to the global. For example, the advance or retreat of the polar ice caps—a global effect with important consequences—depends on how much tiny water molecules move around at a minute level.

Change and movement

Heat is a form of energy that is transferred from one object to another. A hot oven, for example, transfers heat into a cake tin with liquid batter. That transfer warms the batter until it becomes a cake. A room becomes colder in winter when a window is opened, allowing heat to escape outside.

Heat energy is the result of the movement of the tiniest bits of matter—atoms, ions, and molecules—inside liquids, solids, or gases. That energy can flow from one substance to another because of a difference in temperature. So the scientists would say that "heat" is the transfer of "heat energy."

Cold is simply the absence of heat, so when we think that something has become cold, what has really happened is that it has lost heat. Heat transfer takes place constantly—from the changing weather to powering factories, to a melting ice-cream cone.

DID YOU KNOW? In 2019, Russian scientists discovered an 18,000-year-old frozen puppy, with its fur intact. They couldn't decide whether it was a dog or a wolf, but they named it Dogor, a local word for "friend."

Cool Crystals

Some of the most beautiful and expensive objects around us are crystals. These are solid arrangements of atoms or molecules in complicated structures. They are produced through a process that usually involves heat and cooling. That cooling could come from heat radiating from liquid rock or simply from the evaporation of liquids holding a solution. Grow your own crystals in this cool kitchen chemistry experiment.

1. Mix 2 cups of sugar with 1 cup of water in a saucepan.

2. Get your adult to warm the pan, stirring until the sugar dissolves.

3. Ask the adult to pour the liquid into a glass and let it cool.

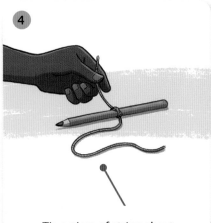

4. Tie a piece of string about 6 in long to the middle of the pencil.

5. Rest the pencil on the rim of the glass, with the string hanging in the liquid.

6. After some days crystals will start to form.

YOU WILL NEED: sugar | water | a glass | string | a pencil

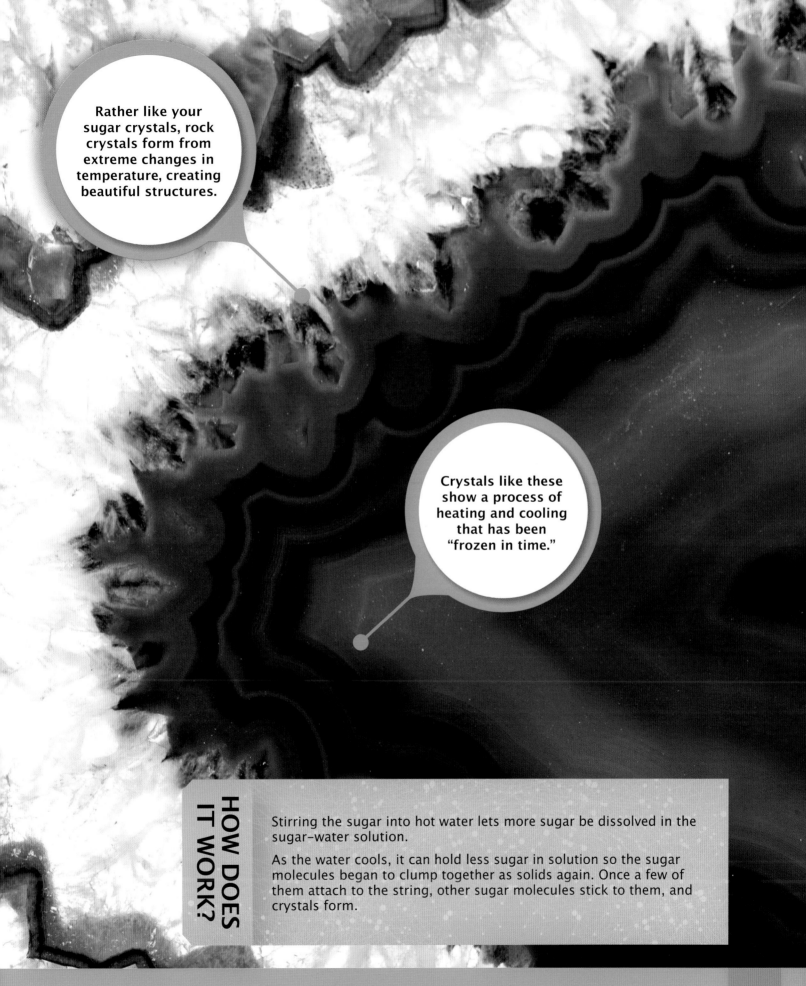

Rather like your sugar crystals, rock crystals form from extreme changes in temperature, creating beautiful structures.

Crystals like these show a process of heating and cooling that has been "frozen in time."

HOW DOES IT WORK?

Stirring the sugar into hot water lets more sugar be dissolved in the sugar–water solution.

As the water cools, it can hold less sugar in solution so the sugar molecules began to clump together as solids again. Once a few of them attach to the string, other sugar molecules stick to them, and crystals form.

DID YOU KNOW? A snowflake is simply a single ice crystal that has formed in a cloud.

All Steamed Up

Water, like all matter, can exist in one of three states: Liquid, solid, or gas. Although pressure can play a part, it is usually the transfer of heat that determines how water moves from one state to another. Freezing (losing heat) and melting (absorbing heat) are linked to water's solid and liquid states. Their gas-related counterparts are condensation (gas to liquid as heat is lost) and evaporation (liquid to gas, or water vapor). Try this experiment on a sunny day when the weather is cool or cold.

Take three drinking glasses and add four ice cubes to each.

Place one on a sunny inside sill and a second in the shade.

Place the third glass on the sill outside the same window.

Leave the three glasses in place for about 30 minutes.

Compare the windows above each glass.

YOU WILL NEED: 3 glasses | ice cubes | a timer

Warm air holds more water (in the form of gas, water vapor) than cold air. The air outside your window is cold, so there's less vapor to condense (and the cubes on the outer sill will melt very little). Inside the heated house, the warm air will melt the cubes and absorb some of the water into vapor. When it touches the glass it condenses, "steaming up" the window with tiny droplets of water. The window by the "shaded" glass has less sunlight to warm it, so less water condenses.

It's easy to draw or write on steamed-up windows by rubbing off the film of water.

Larger drops can also form, as smaller drops stick together, like rain forming in clouds.

DID YOU KNOW? Astronauts on the International Space Station drink water that comes from condensed sweat and breath, which has been filtered along with urine to make it drinkable.

Sharp Focus

Most forms of energy travel from their source in the form of waves—think of light waves or sound waves as good examples. Causing these waves to bend together—for example, through a lens—makes them focus and become more powerful. We can observe that effect when a magnifying glass makes objects seem larger. Focus on this experiment to show how that same lens can magnify other forms of energy. You'll need a sunny day.

1 This experiment depends on solar energy, so make sure to do it on a sunny day.

2 Cut a piece of string about 7 in long.

3 Tie one end to a nut and the other to a cork.

4 Rest the cork so the nut dangles inside a glass bottle.

5 Can you cut the string without touching the bottle?

6 Use the magnifying glass to burn through the string using the sun's rays.

YOU WILL NEED: string | scissors | a cork | a nut | a glass bottle | a magnifying glass

Lasers are instruments that produce concentrated light, which can be focused into very high energies.

Industrial lasers are powerful and precise enough to "burn" letters in hard metals.

HOW DOES IT WORK?

The energy, or radiation, that the sun sends out contains both visible light and heat. When you focus sunlight with the magnifying glass, the lens can concentrate both forms of energy into a small area. That means that the area becomes brighter, but it also means that heat is focused in the same way. And the heat energy, like light, can pass through glass and still have an effect. The focused heat is enough to burn through the thin string.

DID YOU KNOW? Medical lasers enable surgeons to perform extremely delicate operations that would be too risky to do by hand.

Heat Trick

Receptors, or special nerve endings on the skin and in some internal organs, detect heat. Some of them are like alarms to protect against serious damage—in the way we pull back if we touch a hot kettle. Others are programmed to detect changes in outside temperature so the body can regulate itself.

1. Fill a basin with hot water, so that it's about the temperature of a nice, warm bath.

2. Fill a second basin with cold water.

3. Fill a third with a mixture of the two temperatures, somewhere in between.

4. Rest one foot in the "hot" basin and the other in the "cold."

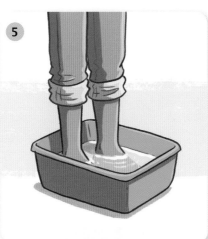

5. Now put both feet in the "in between" basin and see what happens.

Some daring swimmers will jump into these icy waters, even in midwinter.

YOU WILL NEED: 3 basins/tubs | hot, cold, and lukewarm water

HOW DOES IT WORK?

When you step into the "in between" water, the foot from the hot basin will feel cold and the foot from the cold basin will feel warm. That's because the nerves in each foot become "used to" the first temperature—just as you get used to the temperature of a swimming pool. Thermoreceptors (nerve endings that detect temperature changes) in each foot send signals to the brain to say that a basin temperature has become "normal." So, water in the third basin feels warmer than normal for one foot, and colder for the other.

After being outside in the winter air, these brave swimmers will find the water cold but not much colder than the air.

DID YOU KNOW? Swimmers in some Scandinavian and Russian communities insist that plunging into the coldest water is good for the health.

Heat Absorption

Heat is the transfer of a form of energy. How that heat energy is absorbed by (flows into and through) materials differs. It's also linked to how fast heat flows from a substance. We can notice it in large bodies of water. As summer approaches, the air absorbs heat quickly and becomes warm, but water is slower to absorb and remains chilly. Conversely, at the end of the summer, when ocean or lake water is still comfortable for swimming, the air has become colder. Pop a balloon to show how air absorbs heat faster than water.

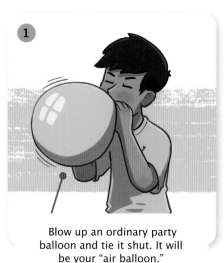

1

Blow up an ordinary party balloon and tie it shut. It will be your "air balloon."

2

Half-fill the second balloon with water and tie it shut.

These lizards can spend hours "soaking up the sun" to gain energy. They move very little, in order to save that energy.

3

Set a lit candle in the bottom of the sink.

4

POP!

Hold the "air balloon" by the flame until it bursts.

5

Then try with the water balloon—it won't burst no matter how close it is.

YOU WILL NEED: 2 balloons | water | a candle

Heat from the candle quickly raises the air temperature enough to burst the first balloon. Water inside the second balloon and nearest the flame also warms up, but it rises away and is replaced by cooler water. That keeps the balloon safely below "bursting temperature."

Make sure that the candle is closest to the bottom of the balloon, so that the water can rise more easily. That will increase your chances of success.

Reptiles bask in the heat of the sun to warm their blood. Mammals, on the other hand, can regulate their own temperatures.

DID YOU KNOW? Animals that need the heat of the sun to warm themselves, like lizards, are called "cold-blooded."

Balloon Boost

Your kitchen can become a testing lab to observe the effect of heat on a gas. Particles inside any heated substance move around more, and if possible, take up more space. And if the same number of particles take up more space, then the gas becomes less dense (since density refers to how much matter a particular volume contains). Less dense fluids and gases usually rise through denser ones, which is why warm air rises. The only scientific tools you'll need here are a freezer and the ceiling—and some party balloons!

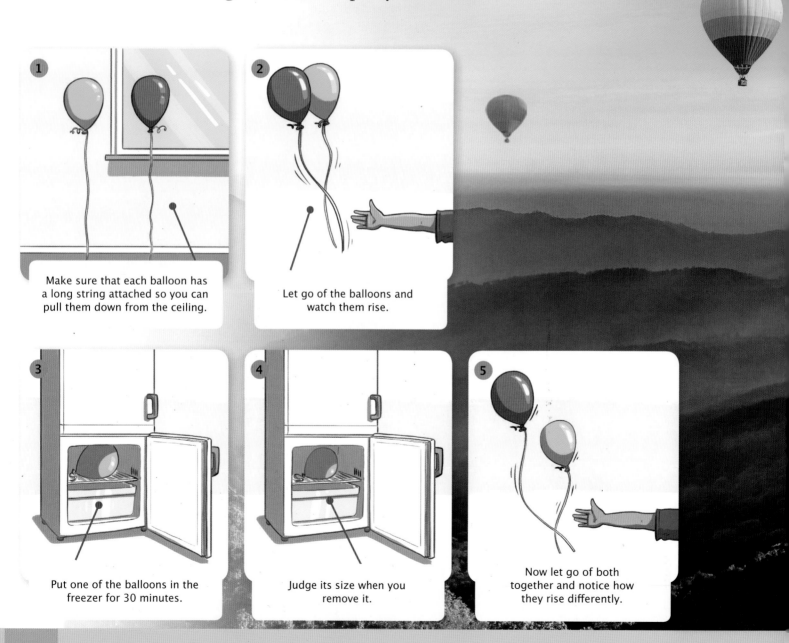

1. Make sure that each balloon has a long string attached so you can pull them down from the ceiling.

2. Let go of the balloons and watch them rise.

3. Put one of the balloons in the freezer for 30 minutes.

4. Judge its size when you remove it.

5. Now let go of both together and notice how they rise differently.

YOU WILL NEED: 2 helium balloons | string

Unlike your helium balloons, hot-air balloons contain ordinary air, so they need to be heated up before they can float up in the sky.

Warming the air inside the balloon makes it less dense, and lighter, than the surrounding air, giving it lift.

HOW DOES IT WORK?

Heat is the movement of particles in a substance, and in your experiment that substance is the helium gas inside the balloon. At room temperature, the helium is less dense than the air outside the balloon—so the balloon floats. Once it has been cooled, the helium particles move more slowly and take up less room inside it. Slower-moving helium molecules take up less space (the balloon shrinks a bit), and the helium becomes denser, so the balloon doesn't float so high.

DID YOU KNOW? The highest hot-air balloon flight was more than twice as high as a commercial airline's altitude.

The Freezing Point

Every substance has a freezing point, when it goes from a liquid state into a solid state. Most of us know the temperatures at which water usually changes state: It is ice (solid) up to 32°F, then liquid, and at 212°F it becomes water vapor (gas). But adding other substances to water can alter the temperature of the phase changes.

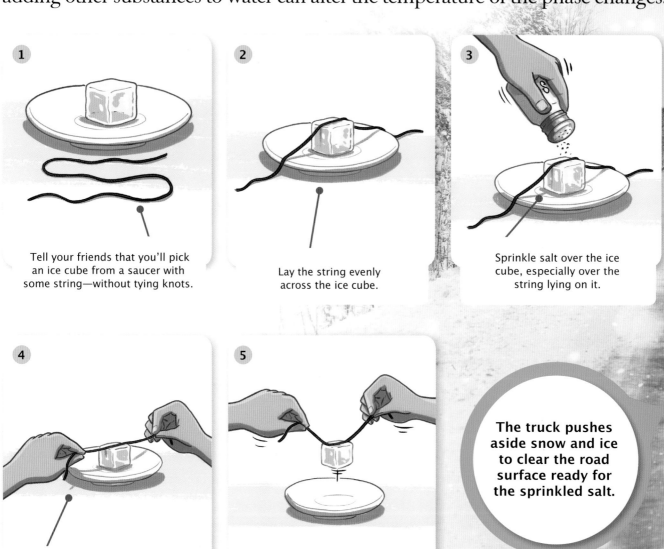

1 Tell your friends that you'll pick an ice cube from a saucer with some string—without tying knots.

2 Lay the string evenly across the ice cube.

3 Sprinkle salt over the ice cube, especially over the string lying on it.

4 Carefully pull both ends of the string so that it's tight.

5 Gently lift the string to pick up the cube.

The truck pushes aside snow and ice to clear the road surface ready for the sprinkled salt.

YOU WILL NEED: an ice cube | a plate | string | salt

Snow-removal trucks sprinkle salt on roads to melt the ice so it is safer to drive.

HOW DOES IT WORK?

Salt water freezes at a slightly lower temperature than pure water. When you sprinkle salt on the ice cube, it melts some of the ice near it, causing the string to rest in a watery gully. But as more ice melts, the salt solution becomes more dilute—and the freezing point creeps up again.

Eventually the water refreezes over the string. This means that you can lift the ice cube thanks to the frozen-in string.

DID YOU KNOW? Using too much salt on winter roads can damage roadside plants. Some American roadsigns warn snow-removal trucks to use less salt.

Particles in Action

This experiment uses colored dye to illustrate the movement of particles through liquids at various temperatures. It is a good experiment to try out a hypothesis, or scientific prediction. Considering all that you've learned so far about heat energy, what do you think the result will be? Test your hypothesis against the result of the experiment—watch those particles in action!

1

Fill one jar with tap water and place it in the fridge for an hour to get really chilled.

2

Fill a second jar with hot water from the tap.

3

Fill a third with mixed hot and cold water.

4

Add three drops of food coloring to each jar.

5

Note the movement of color every 15 seconds for five minutes.

YOU WILL NEED: 3 glass jars | water | food coloring

Two mineral-carrying rivers meet high up in the mountains. Their color reflects the color of the minerals in the water.

Like the chilled water in your experiment, the water in the rivers is cold, so the colors don't blend quickly.

HOW DOES IT WORK?

We know that heat causes particles to move around more quickly in any substance. In the colored dye experiment, the water particles acted as mini spoons—"stirring" the food coloring into solution with the water. The particles in the chilled jar weren't moving around much, so the food coloring didn't mix in very much or very quickly. At the other extreme, though, the hot-water particles were really moving and mixing in the food coloring. And the lukewarm water? Somewhere in between.

DID YOU KNOW? Drops of juice (or blood) can remain undiluted for centuries if they're quickly locked in ice.

Hot Air Power

Warming gases such as air can be very powerful, lifting aircraft or providing the power to propel motor vehicles. In an internal combustion engine (as in many cars), for example, spark plugs cause a constant stream of explosions that cause petrol to expand quickly as a heated gas. The rapid expansion forces pistons to move up and down—"driving" the engine. This experiment demonstrates a less extreme, but still impressive, effect of warming gas. You'll need some adult help—especially the first step, which uses a sharp instrument.

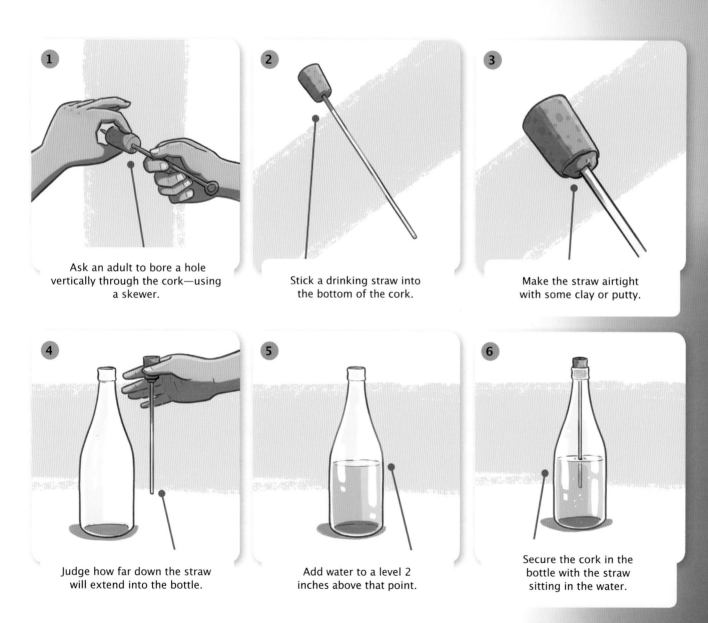

1. Ask an adult to bore a hole vertically through the cork—using a skewer.

2. Stick a drinking straw into the bottom of the cork.

3. Make the straw airtight with some clay or putty.

4. Judge how far down the straw will extend into the bottle.

5. Add water to a level 2 inches above that point.

6. Secure the cork in the bottle with the straw sitting in the water.

YOU WILL NEED: a skewer | a cork | clay/putty | a glass bottle | water

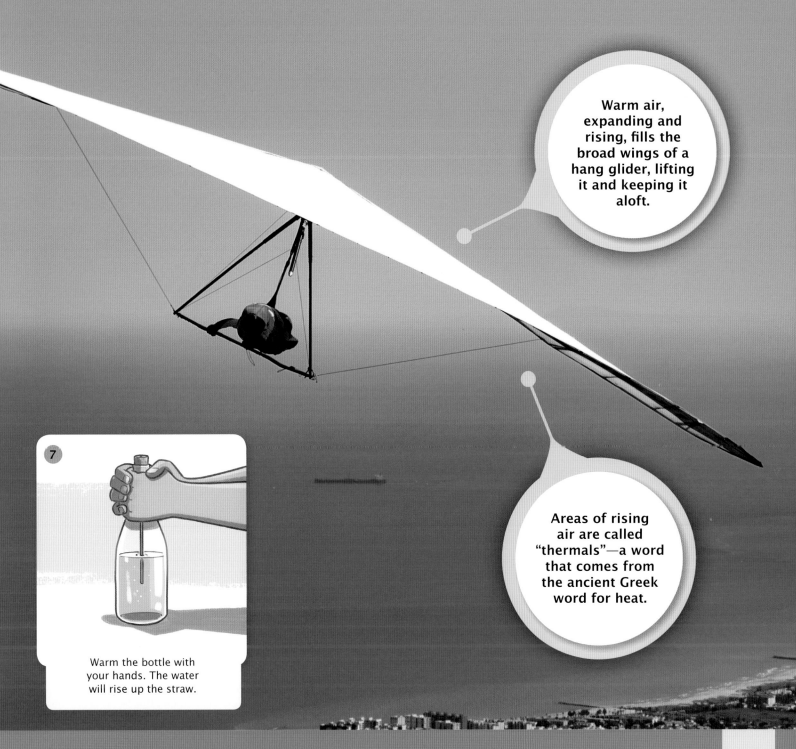

Remember that air warms up quickly. Your hands wrapped around the bottle cause the air inside to warm up. And as the air warms up, it expands. This means that it needs to take up more room—if the bottle's sides were weaker, they would burst under pressure.

Instead, the air pushes down on the surface of the water. As a result, the water needs to go somewhere, so some of it is forced up the straw.

Warm air, expanding and rising, fills the broad wings of a hang glider, lifting it and keeping it aloft.

Areas of rising air are called "thermals"—a word that comes from the ancient Greek word for heat.

7

Warm the bottle with your hands. The water will rise up the straw.

DID YOU KNOW? The pistons that power a car engine move up and down because gas inside them is heated regularly.

Electricity and Magnetism

For centuries people believed that certain stones had magical properties to attract other materials and that lightning was a sign that the gods were angry. Now we know that those stones carry a magnetic charge and that lightning is a form of electricity—but they can still feel uncanny!

Opposites Attract

Both electricity and magnetism involve "opposites attracting." Electricity depends on the attraction between negatively charged particles called electrons and positively charged protons. Magnetic force can attract or repel objects, with magnetic fields having "poles" of attraction at opposite sides.

When scientists began to understand the basics of electricity and magnetism several hundred years ago, they viewed them as separate. We now know that they are part of a wider form of energy called electromagnetism. With that knowledge, engineers have been able to build powerful magnets powered by equally powerful electric forces.

DID YOU KNOW? The Earth is like a giant magnet, with a magnetic field surrounding it. Scientists believe that this magnetic field is generated by electric currents flowing through iron at the planet's core.

Striking Static

Electricity is caused by the flow of electrons (negatively charged particles). Electron flow, called a current, is driven by the attraction of electrons to positively charged protons. In this way, electricity flows from a battery to light a flashlight, or from a wall outlet to power a toaster. But the word "static" means "not moving," so static electricity describes a build-up of a charge (positive or negative) that is not flowing. Static electricity is remarkably powerful, as this striking magic trick demonstrates.

1. Fill the bowl just over halfway with cereal, making sure that it's not tightly packed.

2. Briskly rub the plastic spoon with the woolen hat.

3. Wave the spoon slowly, about 15in over the bowl.

4. Lower the spoon so that it's 2in above the bowl.

5. You will see pieces of cereal start jumping up to the spoon.

YOU WILL NEED puffed rice cereal | a cereal bowl | a plastic spoon | a woolen hat or mitten

Lightning is an extremely powerful form of static electricity, with a massive build-up of negatively charged particles inside clouds.

The negative charge is attracted to positively charged objects below ... and the lightning strikes.

HOW DOES IT WORK?

When you rub the plastic spoon with wool, you generate a negative charge on the spoon's surface. The build-up of this static charge then makes the cereal jump up to the spoon. Opposite charges attract, so positive charges build up on the cereal puffs closest to the spoon, and they jump up. But the charges weaken when the cereal hits the spoon, causing the pieces to become neutral and fall back down.

DID YOU KNOW? Lightning is around 45,000°C—about six times hotter than the surface of the Sun.

Electron Flow

Electricity is all about the flow of electrons in the form of an electrical current. If that current leads back to where it started it is called a circuit. Certain materials (called conductors), which let electrons flow freely, can conduct electricity around a circuit. You can create your own simple circuit to conduct electricity and make a bulb light up in this brilliant experiment.

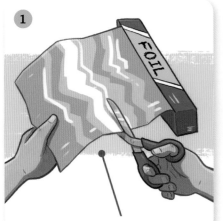

1 Tear a 4 in strip of kitchen foil, making sure the line is straight.

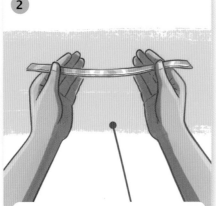

2 Fold the strip over and over along the long side until it's about ½ inch wide.

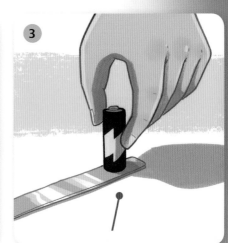

3 Put the battery on one end of the foil and hold it steady.

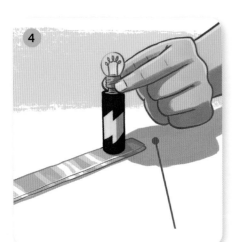

4 Touch the bulb to the top (positive) end of the battery.

5 Hold the bulb in place and touch the other end of the foil to the top of the battery.

6 Now take the end of the foil away from the top of the battery. What happens?

YOU WILL NEED: kitchen foil | a C–size battery | a flashlight bulb

The electrical charge from the battery powered the bulb when you created an electrical circuit with the kitchen foil. At Step 4, the bulb simply rested on the battery—unlit. When the other end of the foil (an excellent conductor) touched the top of the battery, the electrons could pass through the battery and along the foil and back again in a circuit. Some of that flow of electrons was enough to power the light. As soon as you took the foil away from the top of the battery, the circuit was broken and the bulb went out.

Electron flow is also the reason America's famous Statue of Liberty has changed color. It was originally shiny brown.

It gradually changed color as electrons in its copper coating flowed into oxygen in the air around it.

DID YOU KNOW? A pickle will glow and light up if it's connected to a powerful electrical circuit because the salty water inside it is a good conductor.

How to Bend Water

Would you believe that the flow of water from a kitchen faucet can demonstrate the flow of electrons? That's because liquids can be affected by electricity as much as solids. The same principles of opposite charges attracting are at play here. Try this simple experiment—seeing is believing!

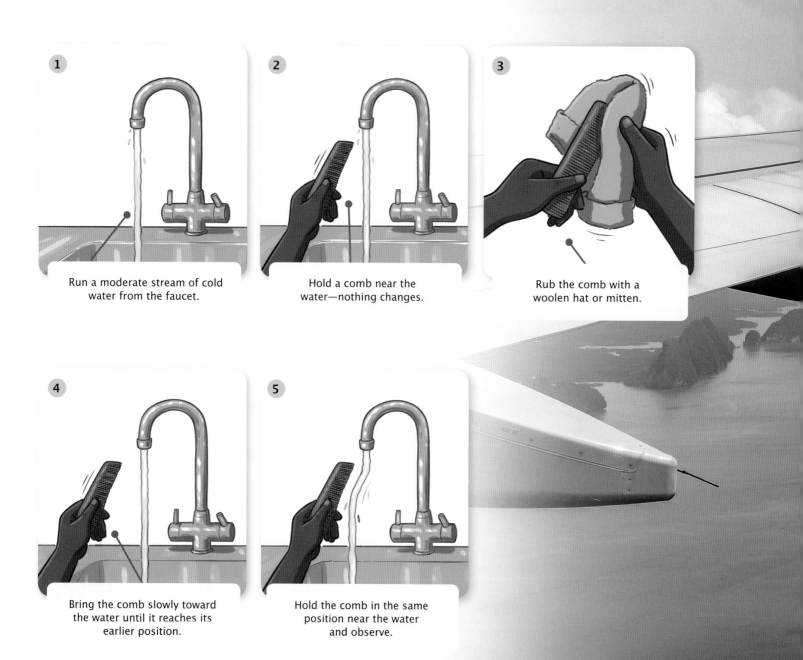

1. Run a moderate stream of cold water from the faucet.

2. Hold a comb near the water—nothing changes.

3. Rub the comb with a woolen hat or mitten.

4. Bring the comb slowly toward the water until it reaches its earlier position.

5. Hold the comb in the same position near the water and observe.

YOU WILL NEED: kitchen tap | a plastic comb | a woolen hat or mitten

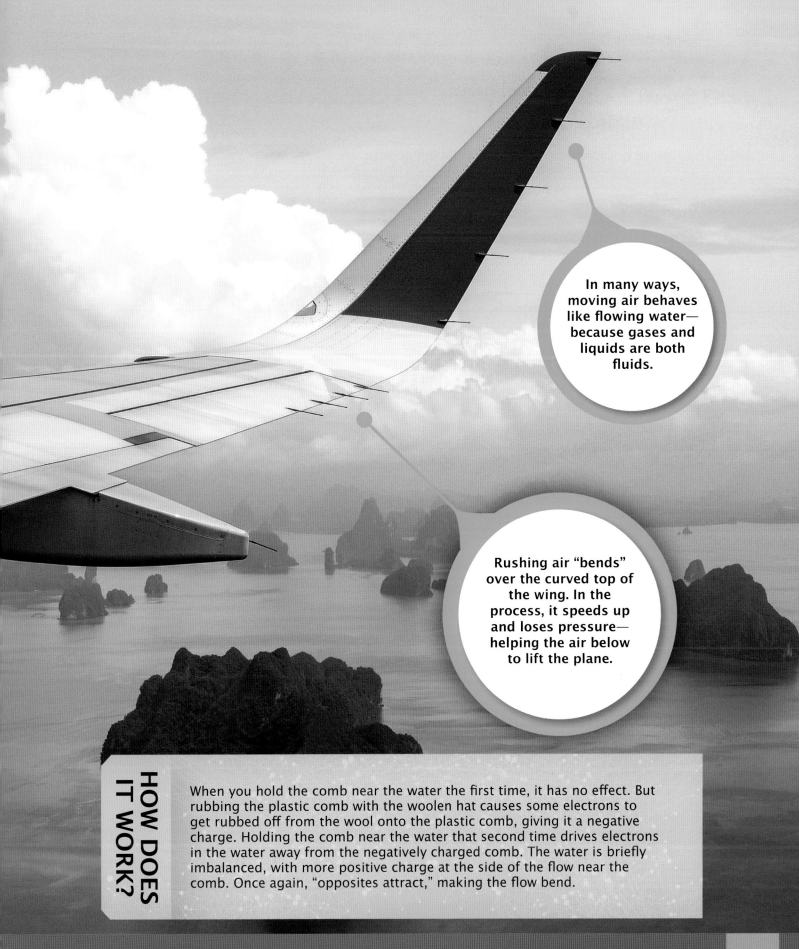

In many ways, moving air behaves like flowing water—because gases and liquids are both fluids.

Rushing air "bends" over the curved top of the wing. In the process, it speeds up and loses pressure—helping the air below to lift the plane.

HOW DOES IT WORK?

When you hold the comb near the water the first time, it has no effect. But rubbing the plastic comb with the woolen hat causes some electrons to get rubbed off from the wool onto the plastic comb, giving it a negative charge. Holding the comb near the water that second time drives electrons in the water away from the negatively charged comb. The water is briefly imbalanced, with more positive charge at the side of the flow near the comb. Once again, "opposites attract," making the flow bend.

DID YOU KNOW? Pure water, created only with hydrogen and oxygen, does not conduct electricity, but it doesn't exist in nature. Most water contains traces of other substances, which are excellent conductors.

Good Conduct

Because electricity is so useful—and potentially dangerous—it's important to be able to tell whether objects can carry an electric charge. In other words, are they good or bad conductors? Instruments called electroscopes detect whether objects are good conductors. It's easy to build your own electroscope and investigate different objects with this experiment.

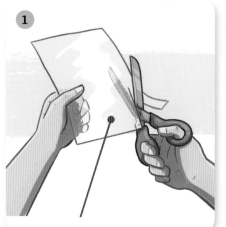

1 Cut two strips of plastic, each about 1 in wide and 7 in long.

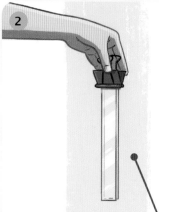

2 Attach a narrow edge of both to the clip so that they hang down.

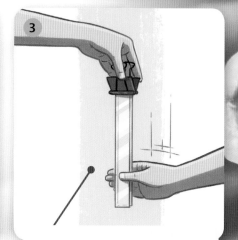

3 Pinch them at the top and slide your hand down the strips quickly.

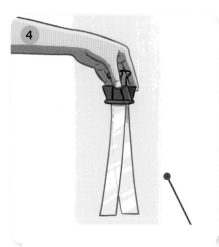

4 Do this two or three more times. The strips will push apart.

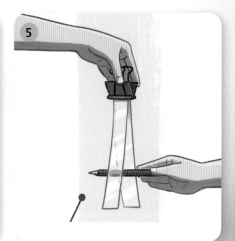

5 Place the pen between the sheets—they'll stay apart.

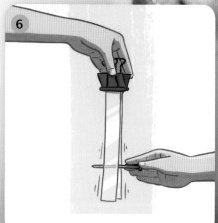

6 Place the nail between the sheets. What happens now?

YOU WILL NEED: scissors | a clear plastic sheet | a bulldog clip | a ball-point pen | a nail

Rubbing the two sheets creates a negative charge, which pushes them apart. The plastic pen is not a good conductor. Its electrons don't move freely, so they remain on the pen's surface and keep the flaps apart.

The metal in the nail, however, is a good conductor. Its electrons move freely, and some move away from the negative flaps. That leaves an imbalance on the nail, which becomes positive. And once again, opposites attract—the positively charged nail attracts the negatively charged plastic, causing the flaps to shut.

Wires made of copper and other metals make good conductors of electrical current.

Wire coverings are made of rubberized plastic or other insulators (materials that don't conduct electricity) for safety reasons.

DID YOU KNOW? Birds can perch safely on overhead power lines because their feet aren't touching any other wires or the Earth—so the strong electrical current passes through them and they aren't electrocuted.

Magnetic Attraction

Gravity and magnetism can sometimes work against each other. The force of gravity pulls objects to other objects of greater mass. On Earth, the mass of the planet itself exerts that force. But a strong enough magnetic field can draw—or repel—objects in the opposite direction to the pull of gravity. Stage your own contest between magnetism and gravity in this experiment, and watch magnetism come out on top.

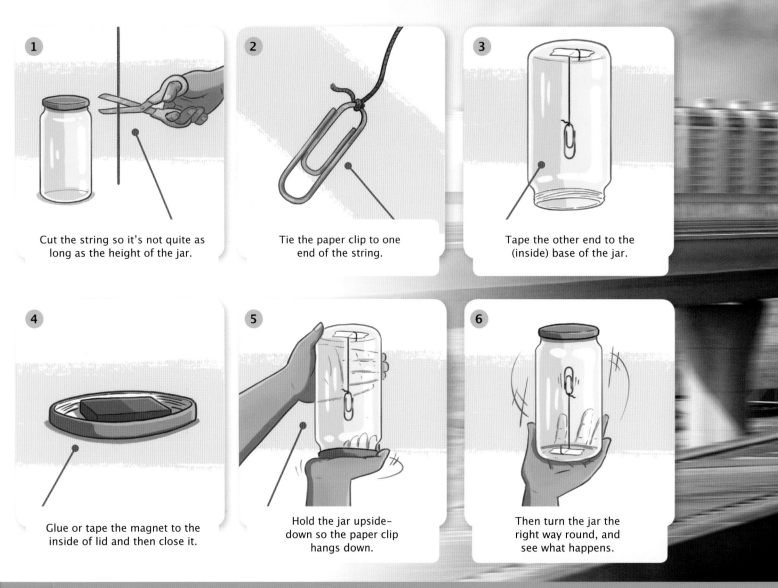

1. Cut the string so it's not quite as long as the height of the jar.

2. Tie the paper clip to one end of the string.

3. Tape the other end to the (inside) base of the jar.

4. Glue or tape the magnet to the inside of lid and then close it.

5. Hold the jar upside-down so the paper clip hangs down.

6. Then turn the jar the right way round, and see what happens.

YOU WILL NEED: string | scissors | a jam jar | a paper clip | tape or glue | a bar magnet

The paper clip is pulled in opposite directions by two different forces. Normally, gravity would pull the clip down, just as anything dropped will fall toward the mass of the Earth. But the magnetic field created by the bar magnet was strong enough to overcome the force of gravity. Of course, that field would be weaker and unable to overcome gravity if the clip were farther away from it. But much more powerful magnetic fields can defy gravity by attracting—or repelling—massive objects.

Like the floating paperclip, Magnetic Levitation (MagLev) trains use magnetism to resist gravity.

The train glides above its tracks because a magnetized coil on the track repels a magnet on the underside of the train.

DID YOU KNOW? The fastest-ever MagLev train reached a speed of 375 mph in 2015 on a test run in Japan. That is 17 mph faster than the record for traditional "wheeled" trains.

Make Your Own Compass

Ships have used magnetic compasses to navigate for centuries, ever since sailors learned that magnetic needles always lined up north–south. We know that is because magnetic fields are aligned in a north–south pattern. The "north" of a compass points to the Earth's magnetic North Pole (which is not the same as the geographic pole that forms the Earth's axis). You can make your own working compass with just a bowl of water and a magnetized needle.

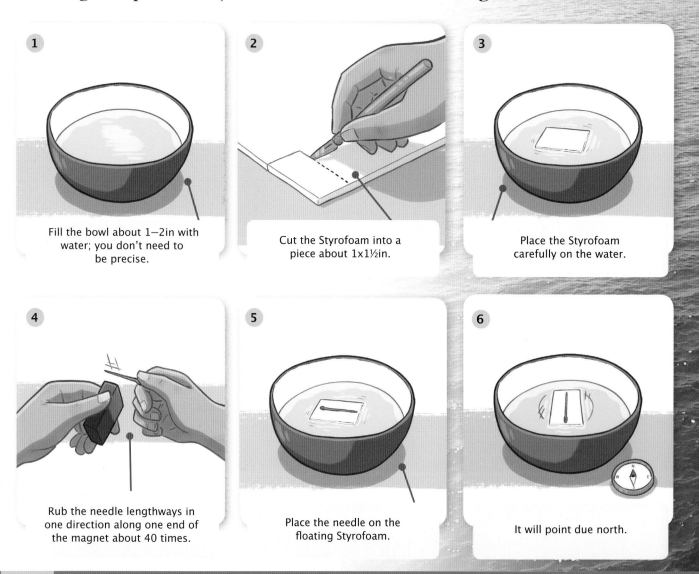

1

Fill the bowl about 1–2in with water; you don't need to be precise.

2

Cut the Styrofoam into a piece about 1x1½in.

3

Place the Styrofoam carefully on the water.

4

Rub the needle lengthways in one direction along one end of the magnet about 40 times.

5

Place the needle on the floating Styrofoam.

6

It will point due north.

YOU WILL NEED a large bowl | Water | Styrofoam | a sewing needle | a bar magnet

Without magnetic compasses, early navigators had to rely on stars to chart their course, which was often difficult in bad weather.

Once ships began to use compasses, the sailors were able to navigate day or night, in any weather.

HOW DOES IT WORK?

In your experiment you see the floating needle slowly turning and then settling into an alignment that points north–south. It has become a compass! The needle would not have reached that alignment if you hadn't rubbed it against the magnet. Objects, especially metal ones, that are rubbed by a magnet can be "magnetized," which means temporarily turned into magnets. Particles that are normally arranged randomly in the metal then line up in one direction, taking on the properties of a magnet.

DID YOU KNOW? The old word for the mineral magnetite was lodestone, meaning "journey, or guiding stone." The name shows how important magnetic compasses became for navigation.

Dynamic Electromagnetism

An electromagnet is produced when electricity and magnetism work together—an electrical current running through a coil creates a magnetic field. The strength of the electromagnet depends on the strength of the current. Ask an adult to help with this experiment, and see how many paper clips a home-made electromagnet can pick up.

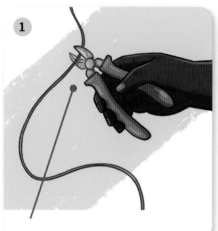

1 Ask an adult to use the wire cutters to snip a 20in length of wire.

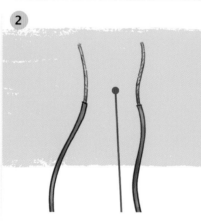

2 About ½in of coating should be stripped from each end of the wire.

3 Wrap 40 loops of the wire tightly around the nail.

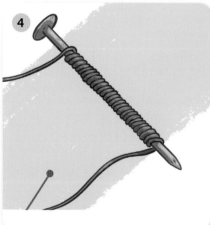

4 Make sure to leave both ends jutting out.

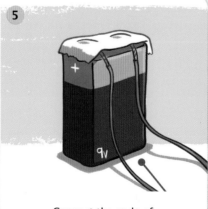

5 Connect the ends of wire to the two battery terminals.

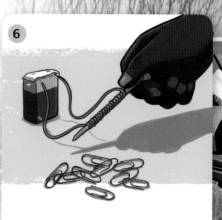

6 Move one end of the nail close to a pile of paper clips and watch what happens.

YOU WILL NEED: insulated wire | wire cutters | a 1in iron nail | a 9–volt battery | paper clips

On a much larger scale than your simple coiled wire, scrapyards use powerful electromagnets to lift heavy metal objects.

Electromagnets can also sift through junk piles to separate magnetic metals (which contain iron and can be lifted) from nonmagnetic metals and other things.

HOW DOES IT WORK?

Your simple coiled wire becomes an electromagnet once it's connected— and the iron core (the nail) becomes magnetic enough to pick up several paper clips at once. The current flows along the wire in a circuit from one battery terminal to the other. As it passes through the coiled section of wire, a magnetic field is created inside the coil. Your electromagnet relies on electricity, and it will lose its magnetic power when either end of the wire is disconnected.

DID YOU KNOW? Space travel in the future might be possible with electromagnetic power: Magnetic fields can accelerate ions (charged particles) to propel spacecraft.

The Invisible Field

A magnetic field is the area around a magnet where there is magnetic force. We can map how a magnet affects neighboring objects—attracting or repelling them—along magnetic field lines. These lines curve and then converge at two ends called poles, where the force is greatest. The Earth's two magnetic poles are at either end (north and south) of the planet's magnetic field. The experiment on this page might be fiddly to do, but it's a good demonstration of the limits of a magnetic field.

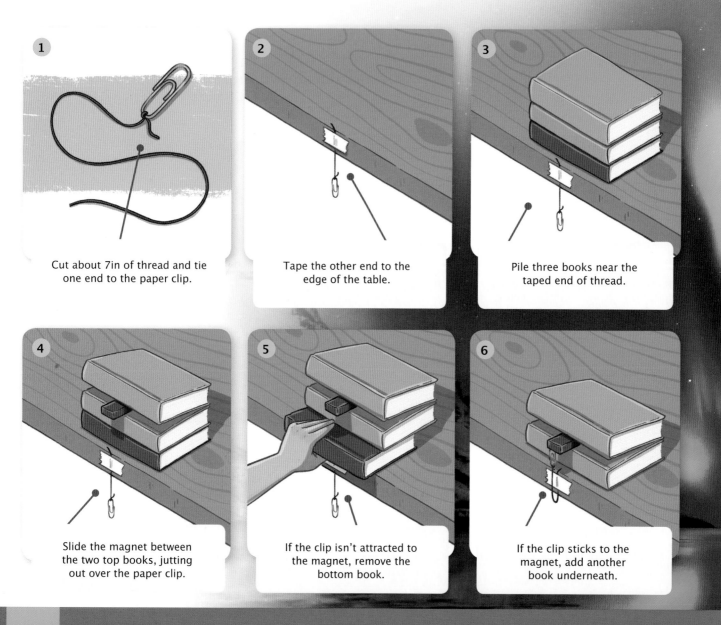

1 Cut about 7in of thread and tie one end to the paper clip.

2 Tape the other end to the edge of the table.

3 Pile three books near the taped end of thread.

4 Slide the magnet between the two top books, jutting out over the paper clip.

5 If the clip isn't attracted to the magnet, remove the bottom book.

6 If the clip sticks to the magnet, add another book underneath.

YOU WILL NEED: thread | a paper clip | tape | 4–6 hardback books | a strong bar magnet | kitchen foil | a cotton sock

This experiment examines both the strength and extent of a magnetic field—the field surrounding the bar magnet. By adding and removing books to find just where the paper clip "floated," you can establish how far the field's strength extendd. But the next phase of the experiment shows that one material (the foil) doesn't disrupt the magnetic field whereas another one (the sock) does. Just as some materials are good electrical conductors, some let magnetic force pass through easily.

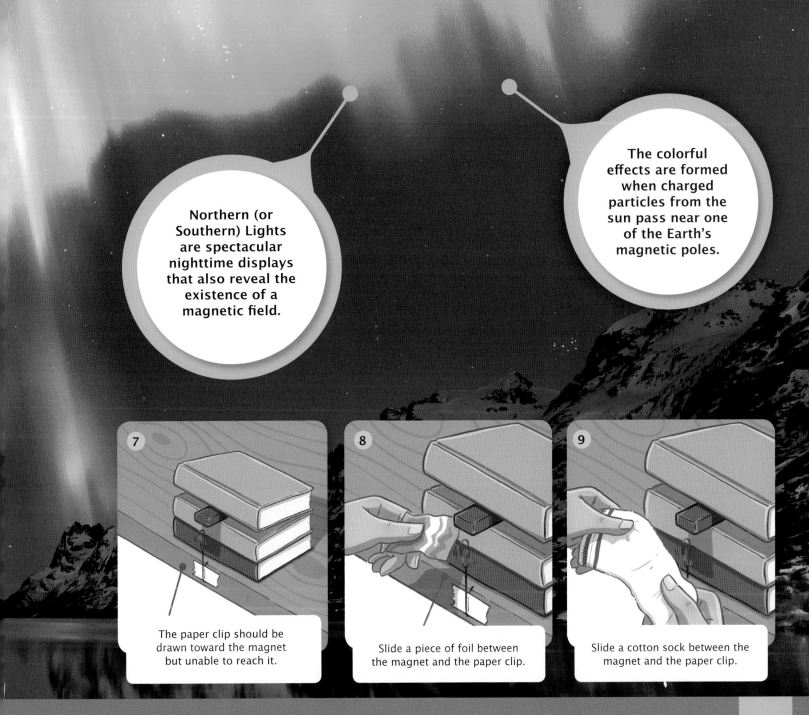

Northern (or Southern) Lights are spectacular nighttime displays that also reveal the existence of a magnetic field.

The colorful effects are formed when charged particles from the sun pass near one of the Earth's magnetic poles.

7 — The paper clip should be drawn toward the magnet but unable to reach it.

8 — Slide a piece of foil between the magnet and the paper clip.

9 — Slide a cotton sock between the magnet and the paper clip.

DID YOU KNOW? The Earth's magnetic poles move about 34–37 miles each year because of magnetic changes in the Earth's core.

Light-Bulb Moment

Old-fashioned light bulbs, of the sort invented by Thomas Edison in the late 1800s, used an electrical current to produce light. The current passed through a thin wire called a filament, which got hot and glowed. Modern lights also use an electrical current, but instead of passing through a wire the electrons bounce around inside the bulb and crash into atoms of gas. Those excitable collisions produce light. And, in this experiment, you can excite the atoms and produce light all by yourself!

1 Blow up the balloon until it's nearly fully blown.

2 Rub the top of the balloon against your hair for 20 seconds.

3 Take the bulb in your other hand.

4 Turn off the lights to make sure it's as dark as possible.

5 Move the balloon quickly back and forth over the bulb. What changes?

6 Hold the balloon steady over the bulb. What happens?

YOU WILL NEED: a balloon | an energy-saving fluorescent light bulb

The outside of the balloon picked up negatively charged electrons from your hair when you rubbed it on your head. Moving the balloon close to the bulb got electrons moving inside the bulb. And they really got moving when you moved the balloon quickly. Those moving electrons collided with mercury vapor, which then emitted ultraviolet light (which we can't see). The ultraviolet light then hit the white material on the coating of the bulb (phosphors). That collision caused the phosphors to emit visible white light, and you saw the bulb light up.

Light bulbs make the night sky sparkle with many different colors in most modern cities.

The color depends on the gas that's inside each bulb—and the colored light that its excited electrons produce.

DID YOU KNOW? People call all colored lights "neon lights," but neon only produces one color: Red. Helium, argon, mercury, and other gases provide the other colors.

105

Living Things

One of the most basic divisions in scientific classification is between living and nonliving things. It's easy to identify some things—such as rocks or seawater—as nonliving. Similarly, no one would mistake a lion, oak tree, or human being for anything other than a living thing.

Shared Qualities

Classification can become a little more confusing, though, when we try to look at everything around us. We can say that all plants and animals are living things, but the category extends much further. Tiny bacteria, mushrooms, and even yeast are also living things.

Scientists define living things as having a number of shared qualities. These include the ability to grow, reproduce, regulate their own systems, and to react to stimuli (actions) around them. As well as these shared characteristics, many living things have developed special qualities of their own. The following pages will shed light on some of those fascinating features.

DID YOU KNOW? According to some studies, zebras developed stripes for protection against harmful horsefly bites.

Sprouting Up

Plants depend on light, carbon dioxide, and water as raw ingredients for photosynthesis, the chemical process by which they produce their own food. They use this food to grow. But does every part of a plant stretch out and grow at the same rate? You'll have a chance to see, by monitoring a growing fava bean in this experiment. It works best if you have a window that receives lots of direct sunlight.

1 Put four fava bean seeds in a bowl and cover with water to soak overnight.

2 Place a wet cotton ball at the bottom of a ziplock sandwich bag.

3 Add more wet cotton balls until they stretch across the base of the bag.

4 Place the seeds evenly across the damp cotton inside the bag.

5 Seal the bag and tape it to the window.

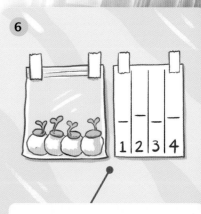

6 Tape some paper up by the bag, marking the seed case and the highest growth.

YOU WILL NEED: 4 fava bean seeds | a bowl | water | cotton balls | a ziplock bag | tape

Your sprouting broad bean will put out shoots that become the stem and the root. If you continue recording the growth of the stem on the paper for a few days, you'll begin to see a pattern. The growth, or elongation, of the stem is really noticeable near the tip and the bit near the seed case remains much the same. That's because plant hormones called auxins become concentrated near the tip of the stem, making the plant cells there more elastic. Becoming more elastic means that they can absorb more water—and stretch.

Bamboo grows as tall as a slender tree, but it's actually a type of grass, which grows in glades resembling huge fields.

Some bamboo species can grow up to 3 ft each day.

7

Continue over several days, noting which section of the stem has lengthened the most.

DID YOU KNOW? The *Puya raimondii* of the Andes in South America takes up to 150 years to flower, and then dies after blooming.

Finding the Light

Light and water are essential for photosynthesis, the chemical process that plants use to produce their own food. Because they need light to survive, plants can be surprisingly active in reacting to it. They grow—and sometimes move during the day—to increase their exposure to it. Plants can even turn corners in their search for light. See for yourself with this clever experiment.

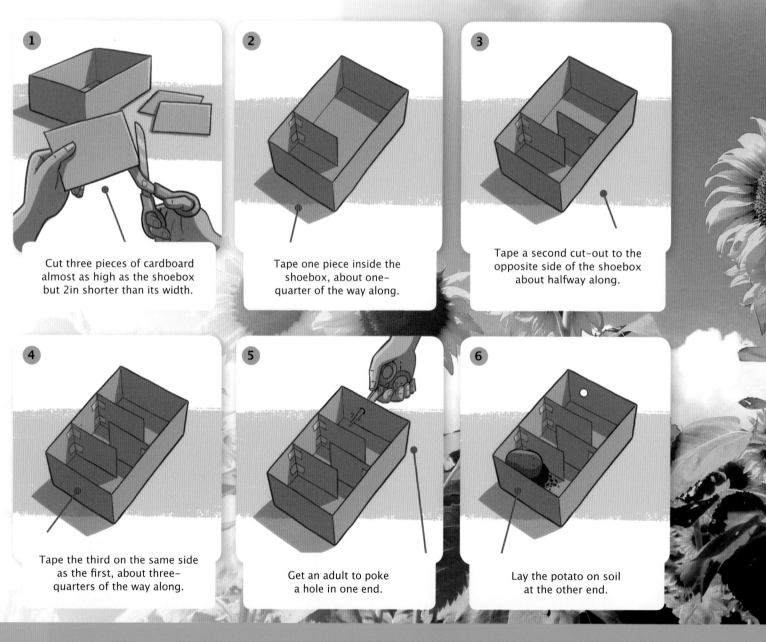

1. Cut three pieces of cardboard almost as high as the shoebox but 2in shorter than its width.

2. Tape one piece inside the shoebox, about one-quarter of the way along.

3. Tape a second cut-out to the opposite side of the shoebox about halfway along.

4. Tape the third on the same side as the first, about three-quarters of the way along.

5. Get an adult to poke a hole in one end.

6. Lay the potato on soil at the other end.

YOU WILL NEED: a shoebox | cardboard | scissors | tape | potting soil | a sprouting potato

HOW DOES IT WORK?

This experiment is an excellent demonstration of phototropism. That's the movement or growth of plants in response to light. Because light is so important to plant food production, plants seek it out. Auxin, the chemical that encourages cell growth, becomes concentrated on the side of the plant stem farther from the light. The stem grows faster on that side, helping the plant turn corners as it reacts to the light. In this case, the plant sensed the light coming from each tiny hatch.

Like the sprouting potato, other plants respond to light, too. Sunflowers live up to their name by the way they grow.

Growing sunflowers face the sun and slowly turn each day as they follow its course.

7

Cover the shoebox and place it near a light source.

8

Check every few days but cover again each time.

DID YOU KNOW? Plants also use other "tropisms" to respond to gravity and to sense where to find water.

Chemical Defense

Most living things have an outside layer to protect them. Chemical substances called acids can pierce this outside layer by eating away at it. Even the things we eat and drink contain acids that can damage the hard surface of our teeth if we don't keep them clean. Scientists can use other chemical substances to protect against those damaging attacks. This thought-provoking experiment uses eggshell to show how damaging acids can be, and why we need defense.

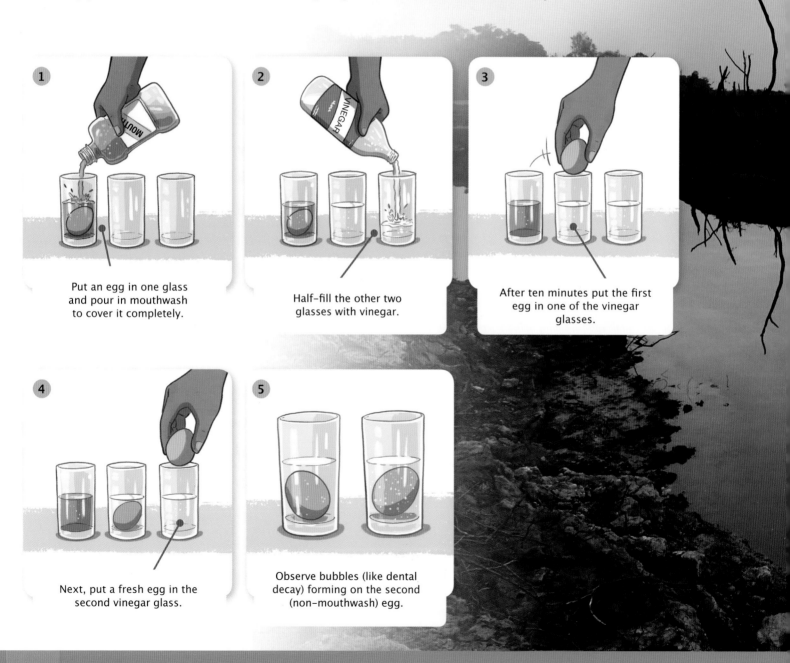

1. Put an egg in one glass and pour in mouthwash to cover it completely.

2. Half-fill the other two glasses with vinegar.

3. After ten minutes put the first egg in one of the vinegar glasses.

4. Next, put a fresh egg in the second vinegar glass.

5. Observe bubbles (like dental decay) forming on the second (non-mouthwash) egg.

YOU WILL NEED: 3 drinking glasses | 2 eggs | fluoride mouthwash | vinegar

Trees and other plants have even less defense than eggshells or teeth. They can be damaged or killed by acid.

Fewer trees means there aren't roots holding the soil together, so it is harder for new life to grow as the soil is eroded away.

HOW DOES IT WORK?

Eggshell is made of a substance called calcium carbonate. It's like your teeth, where the hard outer layer of enamel also contains calcium compounds. Many acids, such as the acetic acid in vinegar (or the acids in many types of soda), react with compounds like calcium carbonate. You saw that with the bubbles forming on one of the eggs. Chemicals that contain fluoride are used in mouthwash and help to reverse some of those chemical reactions, allowing the calcium carbonate to rebuild, or "remineralize." Fluoride mouthwash or toothpaste protect teeth from acids in this way.

DID YOU KNOW? Some communities add fluoride to drinking water to promote dental health.

X-ray Vision

Doctors and other medical specialists use X-ray imaging to get clear pictures of what lies beneath a patient's skin—without having to actually look inside the body. The X-rays pass through skin and muscles, but when they meet obstacles such as bones they show up clearly as shadows. You can use a flashlight like an X-ray machine and see your own bones in this experiment—but you'll need a very dark room for it to work.

1. Turn off any lights and draw the curtains to get the room really dark.

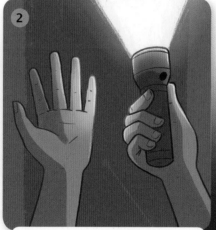

2. Check your flashlight is shining brightly.

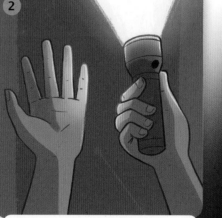

3. Hold the flashlight up to the palm of your free hand.

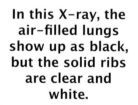

4. Press the flashlight against the palm—your bones appear as they do on an X-ray image.

In this X-ray, the air-filled lungs show up as black, but the solid ribs are clear and white.

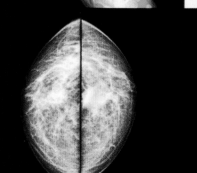

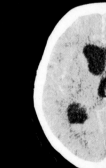

YOU WILL NEED: a flashlight (the end should be narrower than the width of your hand) | dark room

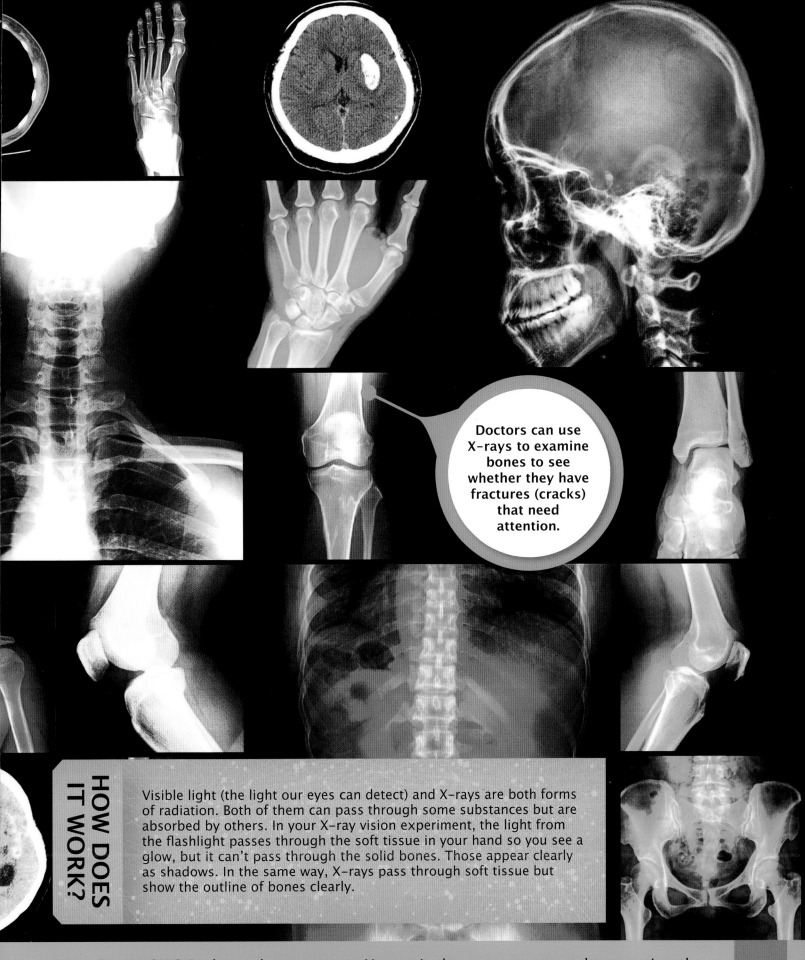

Doctors can use X-rays to examine bones to see whether they have fractures (cracks) that need attention.

HOW DOES IT WORK?

Visible light (the light our eyes can detect) and X-rays are both forms of radiation. Both of them can pass through some substances but are absorbed by others. In your X-ray vision experiment, the light from the flashlight passes through the soft tissue in your hand so you see a glow, but it can't pass through the solid bones. Those appear clearly as shadows. In the same way, X-rays pass through soft tissue but show the outline of bones clearly.

DID YOU KNOW? Prolonged exposure to X-rays is dangerous, so people operating the equipment need to stand behind protective barriers.

Membrane Management

All living organisms, whether plants or animals, depend on a range of liquids for nourishment or growth. Some of those liquids flow through channels, like our veins. Permeable tissue allows nearly all liquid through, but semipermeable tissue slows the flow to keep things controlled. Cellophane, which is semipermeable, acts like a cell membrane in this experiment to show how liquids pass through.

1. Fill a drinking glass with water.

2. Stir in 1 teaspoon of salt until it's dissolved.

3. Stir in several drops of food dye into a bowl of water until the liquid is colored.

4. Cut a cellophane circle wider than the rim of your glass.

5. Cover the glass with the cellophane and secure tightly with a rubber band.

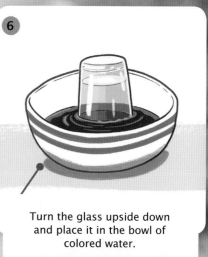

6. Turn the glass upside down and place it in the bowl of colored water.

YOU WILL NEED: a drinking glass | water | a teaspoon | salt | a small bowl | food dye | cellophane | scissors | a rubber band

You'll see the water in the glass gradually gain some of the color from the dyed liquid in the bowl. That's because the cellophane (which is made from cellulose, an important ingredient of plants) is slightly permeable, letting a limited flow of liquid pass through it. In that way, it's acting just like a cell membrane in the way a variety of liquid particles can pass into (and from) cells.

Cell membranes inside growing grapes let water and nutrients pass into all the cells.

The grape's outer skin is not very permeable, so moisture is kept inside as the grape ripens.

7

After some time the water in the glass should become colored as well.

DID YOU KNOW? The permeability of grape skins enables water to be released as they dry to become raisins.

Natural Navigation

It's possible to find your way through unfamiliar countryside if you understand some basic scientific principles. Even without GPS or a traditional compass, you can work out which way is north (and so the other directions) through careful observation. Learn how to use a mossy tree trunk to navigate naturally in this outdoor experiment.

Lay the compass on the ground next to the first tree.

Check that the compass is pointing north.

Walk around the tree to find the side with the most moss.

The "mossy" side should be the side that faces north. Repeat the steps to find the mossiest tree.

The thickest growth of moss is on the shadier, north side of the tree, where nourishing moisture also collects.

YOU WILL NEED: hand-held compass | 3 trees with moss growing at their base

Moss likes to grow on dying or dead trees in woodlands.

HOW DOES IT WORK?

It's possible to navigate naturally in this way because some delicate plants are damaged by strong sunlight. They thrive in shadier conditions. Moss is one of those plants, growing best where it's pointing away from the sun. In the Northern Hemisphere, the sun appears in the southern sky, so that the northern side of a tree is usually shadier—and an indication of which way is north. The same principle applies in the Southern Hemisphere, where moss prefers the southern side of trees.

DID YOU KNOW? Many healthy trees are "lopsided," with the side facing the sun growing more branches and leaves.

Living Leaves

In some ways a plant is like a mini-plumbing system, with water constantly flowing into it, through it, and finally from it. The plant's roots draw water and nutrients from the soil. The water and nutrients flow through the plant, nourishing tissue along the way. The water then enters the air through the leaves. That flow pulls even more water from the ground, and the process continues. Watch a living leaf in action in this experiment—and don't forget to remove the plastic bag afterward!

1 Find a leaf about the size of your hand, or even a bit bigger

2 Cover the leaf with the plastic bag.

3 Seal the bag tight against the branch by looping and twisting the rubber band.

4 Check the bag after 15 minutes: It should have become cloudy.

5 Check again after 24 hours: Water should have collected.

6 Make sure to remove the bag afterward, so the leaf isn't harmed!

YOU WILL NEED: a large leaf on a tree or shrub | clear plastic bag (like a sandwich bag) | a rubber band

All living leaves lose water in this way, so a wooded hillside is like a pump—constantly sending water into the air.

Some of the escaped water vapor has condensed to form fog or clouds hanging over this woodland.

HOW DOES IT WORK?

Normally we wouldn't notice the water that has left a plant because it becomes water vapor, an invisible gas. But in this experiment, that gas collects inside the plastic bag and then, as the temperature decreases, the gas turns back into liquid water through condensation (the opposite of evaporation). The plant needs to let the water escape so that more water can be drawn up from the ground and this process of transpiration can continue.

DID YOU KNOW? Cacti and other desert plants have thick, hard leaves to limit how much water is lost to the scorching heat.

Muscle Memory

Every action we do involves a set order of tensing and relaxing muscles. When we learn to do something very complicated, like learning to ski or to play a musical instrument, we need to repeat the action over and over again. Eventually (if we're lucky) we can do the action without thinking about it. That unconscious learning is called muscle memory, although it's really about the brain telling the muscles what to do. Have fun demonstrating muscle memory to your friends with this simple experiment.

Ask one friend to stand in the doorway, with one arm hanging straight down along one side of the doorway.

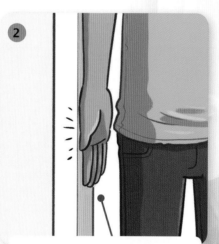

Have them press an arm really hard against the doorframe.

Count to 30 and ask your friend to walk away.

Their "pressed" arm should rise up slowly—and automatically and surprisingly.

Ask your second friend to do the same thing, but count to only 15 this time.

Compare to see whose arm rose the highest.

YOU WILL NEED: a doorway | 2 volunteers | a stopwatch/clock

The rising–arm experiment experiment is a very basic demonstration of muscle memory. It doesn't involve a complicated series of actions. Instead, it's one action that is constantly being repeated and reinforced in the brain. So the brain responds by sending out a message to push hard, even after the obstacle (the doorframe) has been removed. The result is the person's arm continuing to push— and slowly rise. The second friend's arm won't rise so dramatically, because they pressed for a shorter time.

Stiltwalkers practice with small stilts until their arms and legs have developed muscle memory.

That muscle memory gives them the confidence and skill to balance on bigger stilts— and to try more complicated moves like dancing!

DID YOU KNOW? Muscle memory can also be bad. If you've learned to serve the wrong way in tennis, for example, then it's hard to "unlearn" that habit.

Proof of Life

All living organisms need nutrition in order to grow and stay healthy. Most nutrients are combined with other substances, so organisms need to break down (digest) those substances to nourish themselves. Digestion is a chemical process and the material that isn't used for food is discharged as waste. And that waste, in turn, might nourish other organisms. Different living organisms produce different kinds of waste, and this experiment uses one kind to blow up a balloon!

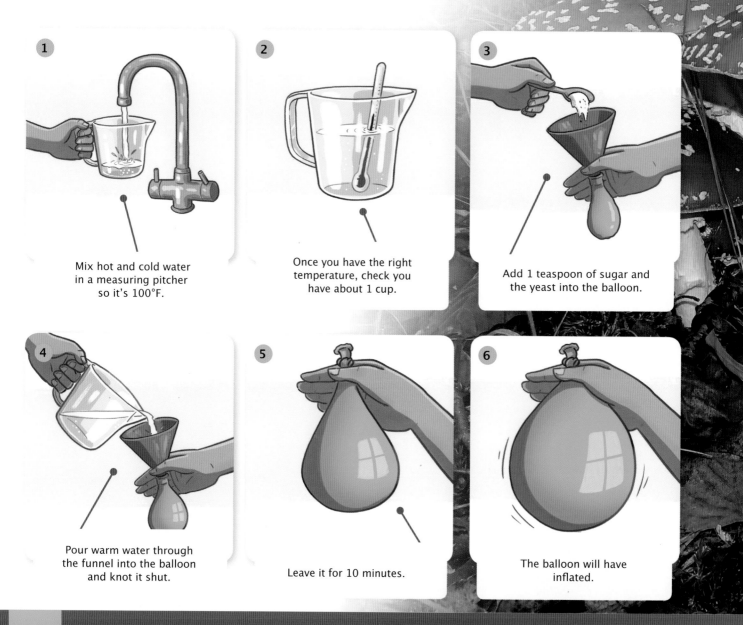

1. Mix hot and cold water in a measuring pitcher so it's 100°F.

2. Once you have the right temperature, check you have about 1 cup.

3. Add 1 teaspoon of sugar and the yeast into the balloon.

4. Pour warm water through the funnel into the balloon and knot it shut.

5. Leave it for 10 minutes.

6. The balloon will have inflated.

YOU WILL NEED: a measuring pitcher | water | a thermometer | sugar | a teaspoon | a packet of yeast | a balloon | a funnel

Yeasts and mushrooms, like these toxic toadstools, are all fungi. Mushrooms get most of their nutrition from the decayed bits of vegetation.

Like other fungi, mushrooms don't need light to make food and grow, because they are not plants.

HOW DOES IT WORK?

Yeast is a living organism, and a relative of mushrooms. This experiment creates the conditions for yeast to be nourished and to digest food. The warm water made it easier for the yeast to absorb and digest the sugar (its food).

Just as animals burp while digesting food, the yeast also gives off a gas (in this case carbon dioxide) while it digests the food. And that's what fills the balloon.

DID YOU KNOW? One huge colony of mushrooms in Oregon is thought to be 8,500 years old.

Glossary

ABSORB
To take in or soak up through chemical or physical action.

ACID
A sour-tasting chemical substance that can dissolve some solids, including metals.

ACID RAIN
A solution of rainwater and acid (from atmospheric pollution) that can have harmful effects on aquatic animals and plants, and damage buildings.

ADHESION
The sticking together of particles of different substances.

AMPLIFY
To increase the strength of energy travelling in waves.

ANGULAR MOMENTUM
The inertia of an object rotating on an axis (spinning).

BERNOULLI PRINCIPLE
The observation that the pressure inside a moving fluid (liquid or gas) decreases as the velocity of that fluid increases.

BUOYANCY
An upward-pushing force that can allow an object to float on a fluid.

CENTER OF MASS
The point at which there is an equal amount of an object's mass either side of it.

CHARGE
A measure of the flow of electrons, either positive or negative.

CIRCUIT
The closed path that an electrical current follows.

COHESION
The sticking together of particles of the same substance.

COLLOID
A mixture of particles of one substance suspended in another substance.

COMPASS
A navigational aid that uses a magnetized needle to point north.

CONDENSATION
The process of changing from a gas to a liquid.

CONDUCTOR
A material that allows energy to flow through it.

CONSERVATION OF MOMENTUM
The total momentum of a system (for example, objects moving toward each other) at one time remains the same at a later time.

CONTRACT
Become smaller.

CRYSTAL
A solid substance whose molecules are arranged in regular, repeating shapes.

CURRENT
The rate of flow of an electrical charge past a certain point.

DECAY
To rot or deteriorate, usually because of the action of bacteria or microscopic organisms.

DENSITY
The amount of mass contained in a specific volume of a substance.

DIGEST
To break down a substance into the parts that make it up.

DISPLACE
Force away from a particular place.

DISSOLVE
To become absorbed into a liquid to form a solution.

DOPPLER EFFECT
The increase or decrease in the frequency of radiation as the source of the radiation moves toward or away; the pitch of a sound rises or falls depending on the direction of that movement.

ELECTROMAGNETIC
A type of energy that can take many forms and which operates in tandem with magnetic forces.

ELECTRON
A negatively charged particle that forms part of an atom.

ENERGY
The power or ability to make something work or be active; energy takes many forms, including chemical, electrical, and thermal.

EXCITED
Having become more active.

EXPAND
To occupy more space.

EXTRACT
To remove or take out.

FOCAL POINT
The point where waves or rays meet after refraction or reflection.

FOCUS
To move or adjust to radiation to concentrate it on a focal point.

FORCE
Strength or power used on an object.

FRACTURE
To break (as in a fractured bone).

FREEZING POINT
The temperature at which a liquid becomes a solid.

FREQUENCY
A measure (for example, in radiation) of how many waves are travelling in a set time, such as a second.

FRICTION
A force that acts against motion between objects.

GRAVITY
A force that causes objects to be attracted to each other.

INERTIA
The tendency of an object that is not moving to stay still, or of a moving object to continue to move—unless an outside force acts on it.

INSULATOR
A substance that slows or stops the passage of radiation.

LAMINATE
Made of layers of material bonded together.

LASER
A concentrated beam of light (or other form of electromagnetic radiation).

MAGLEV
An engineering method, short for "magnetic levitation," that uses a basic principle of electromagnetic force to lift or separate massive objects.

MAGNETIC FIELD
An area near a magnetic or electromagnetic force in which a magnet can exert magnetic force.

MAGNETIC POLE
One of the two points in a magnetic field where lines of magnetic force are either drawn together or spread out.

MAGNETISM
A process linked to electrical charge which leads to objects either being drawn toward or away from each other.

MASS
The amount of matter that any substance contains.

MEMBRANE
A thin sheet of tissue or layer of cells acting as a boundary within an organism.

MOLECULE
A group of atoms bonded together.

MOMENTUM
The mass of a moving object multiplied by its velocity (speed).

NATURAL GAS
A flammable (burnable) gas that occurs naturally and has a similar chemical make-up to oil.

NOURISHMENT
The food that is necessary for health and growth.

PERMEABLE
Allowing water or other liquids to pass through.

PHOTOSYNTHESIS
The method that plants use to produce their own food, using sunlight to trigger a chemical reaction between carbon dioxide and water.

PHOTOTROPISM
The way in which a plant changes the direction it is pointing depending on where the sun is.

POLYMER
A substance with a molecular structure built up of similar units bonded together.

POROUS
Having many small openings (pores) through which water and other liquids can flow.

PRESSURE
Force that is applied to the surface of an object.

RADIATION
The process in which energy is transmitted in waves or particles.

REACT
To undergo a chemical reaction.

REACTION
A chemical change produced by two or more substances coming into contact with each other; the meeting usually changes all the substances.

RECEPTOR
An organ or cell that can detect an outside stimulus (such as light or heat) and can transmit the information through the nervous system.

REFLECT
To send back energy (such as light or heat) without absorbing it.

REFRACTION
The change in direction of a ray of light or other form of energy as it passes through some substances.

RESONANCE
Contact with another vibration of the same frequency can produce a much greater vibration.

SOLUTION
The process in which a solid, gas, or liquid is dispersed (spread out) evenly through another solid, gas, or liquid.

STATE (OF MATTER)
The structure of a form of matter— usually solid, liquid, or gas.

STATIC ELECTRICITY
A stationary electric charge that builds up on an insulating material, as when electrons are rubbed onto wool.

SURFACE TENSION
The attraction of particles on the surface of a liquid, forming an elastic film across the surface.

THERMAL
A rising column of warm air.

THERMAL EXPANSION
The way in which matter changes its shape in response to a change in temperature.

TRANSPIRATION
The passage of water through a plant, from being absorbed by the roots until it passes through the leaves by evaporation.

VOCAL CORDS
Folds of tissue stretched across the throat, which vibrate to produce sound as air passes through them.

WATER VAPOR
The gas form of water.

WAVELENGTH
The distance between waves of radiation.

X-RAYS
High-energy radiation with a short wavelength that is able to pass through materials which ordinary (visible) light cannot; X-ray images are valuable medical tools.